THE FAITH EXPERIMENT

YOUR PERSONAL FAITH JOURNEY TO
WALKING ON THE WATER WITH JESUS

THE FAITH
EXPERIMENT

JOSH AMSTUTZ

-THANKS-

This book would never have come together without many talented and gracious individuals.

Once again, I want to thank Barb Krause for taking us on the journey from manuscript to production. You are a joy to work with, a brilliant editor, and such a gift to myself and Lakeland. To Heather Koepke, thanks again for your attention to details, your willingness to dive into this project and your gifts that make it better. To Kelly Burmeister, you've rocked it in taking this project through all the hoops and to completion. Way to go! To Richard Holt and the Lakeland's Overseers thanks for making a way for me to tackle my dreams and making them a reality. Thanks to Arol McFadden, you are one amazing artist and Paul Gaul in helping with the cover design. And thanks again to Life Together for their book design format, you've always been a great partner in seeing the local church produce the highest quality discipleship materials.

And to my wife Lisa, thank you from the bottom of my heart. I love you so much. This book was really a labor of love, not just from me, but also from you as you carried our home for the many weeks I took in writing it. To my kids, thanks for just living life…you make my life rich and give me an endless supply of illustrations.

I pray that out of all our efforts there will be many who push their faith to the extreme and discover a God who is bigger, better, and more amazing than we could ever think or imagine.

TABLE OF CONTENTS

INTRODUCTION

What's your favorite Christmas movie? Is it "White Christmas," "Miracle on 34th Street," "It's a Wonderful Life," "The Polar Express," "Rise of the Guardians," "Elf," "The Grinch," "The Santa Clause" or another? Some are simply fun movies that take place during Christmas, like "White Christmas," but then there are the vast majority of others that lean into an entirely different category.

That category is one of faith or belief. Think about it. In "The Polar Express," you have a young boy who is struggling to believe in Santa. And the epitome of that belief is signified by his ability to hear the ringing of Santa's sleigh bells. Until he believes, he can't hear. Or in "Elf," where Santa's sleigh, powered by humanity's belief in Santa, no longer flies because of the lack of believers. Or in "Rise of the Guardians," when humanity's belief in the Easter Bunny, the Tooth Fairy, Santa, and Jack Frost diminishes, their power against the villain Pitch Black also diminishes.

Most of these movie plots center around the same concept: belief and faith. If only there was stronger belief or stronger faith, then the crisis would be averted. And good ultimately wins only when pure, whole and honest belief is displayed.

It's interesting that so many movies actually center around the concept of faith. Even in an action film like "The Matrix," the movie rises and falls along with the main characters' engagement in their faith. Morpheus believes that Neo is "The One." The Oracle says Neo is not "The One." Does Trinity love him? Because that would be an indicator that he is "The One." Does Neo believe he is "The One"? Do you see it in there? Who believes? And who does not believe?

Now I've just given you a long list of movies that you've got to go watch. Enjoy ... and you're welcome. But the point is, our world is actually obsessed with belief and faith.

Is it possible that this fixation on belief and faith is not by accident?

Is it possible that scripture is true? And that "... He has also set eternity in the human heart;" (Ecclesiastes 3:11) ... that creation points us to a creator (Romans 1:20) ... that we are made in the image of God (Genesis 1:27) ... that we are made for Him (Colossians 1:16) and as a result of all that, there is a longing for belief and faith within all of us. And that longing within us is simply longing to get out of us.

In each of the Christmas movies, it all boils down to the amount of faith in the individual. There is always a level of faith that has the ability to grow and produce something MORE.

This journey of faith may be the biggest hurdle we consistently wrestle with. You may wonder, if things are going poorly in my life, is that a reflection of my faith? If something good happens, is that a reflection of my faith? When I pray for something, is my faith making a difference? If I sinned earlier in the day, is my faith currently diminished? Are there things that are too big for my faith? What if I pray for something, but I'm doubting in my head; did I negate my faith? What if I don't claim to be a Christian, can I have faith? Can my faith impact anything?

As you can see, there are many aspects to faith, numerous questions you might have, and a whole lot of uncertainties around your faith.

Yet, I think most would like to grow in their faith.

Now before I get too far, you might be thinking, "I don't even claim to have faith." Well, it may be true that your faith in God is near non-existent, or perhaps, just at the beginning stage. But I would argue **you are on a faith journey.**

I've always likened the faith journey to a wide continuum. At one end of the spectrum, you might have someone who personally identifies as **far from God**. They may even say they hate God, don't believe in God, or want nothing to do with God. That's fine, that's where they are at, but I personally believe they are still on the faith spectrum. They are simply far from Him in their faith. On the other end of the spectrum you've got the individual who is close to God, whose faith is active, and whose life is impacted in every single way because of their faith.

Those are the two extremes. And right in the middle is the cross. The cross represents salvation and faith in Jesus. Not faith in myself or my good works, or anything I could do, but faith in what He did to pay for my sins at the cross. When I place my faith in Jesus, He becomes my Lord, my Savior…and as scripture says it, "The old has gone, the new is here!" (2 Corinthians 5:17).

On this side of the cross, my faith is now working in a new way. It doesn't mean that prior to faith in Christ I had no faith, it means my faith was simply in an exploratory stage…and that's okay, that's where everyone has to start. Everyone has to explore faith at some point. Perhaps one of the benefits of hopping into this journey is that this book will help you explore your faith in new ways. No matter which side of the cross you consider yourself to be on, I would encourage you to take a step in your journey: take a step of faith.

The Faith Experiment is a journey that will lead each and every one of us to examine aspects of faith that the Bible talks about.

There are over 400 verses in the Bible that mention the word faith or belief. We read about individuals who exercise faith. We read about Jesus talking about faith. We see the power of faith in the amazing stories in the Bible. And within it all, we see thematic elements that seem to influence faith. We see elements that grow faith, we see things that stunt faith, we see individuals that use faith, some who abuse faith, some who run **to** faith and others that run **from** faith. The point is, there is a lot for us to learn about and grow in, in the area of faith.

You might ask why? Why bother growing in your faith?

Hebrews 11:6 says, "And without faith it is impossible to please God, because anyone who comes to him must believe that he exists and that he rewards those who earnestly seek Him."

If this verse is true, that's why we should bother. I want to come to the end of my life and hear God say to me, "Well done, good and faithful servant." Those are the words Jesus repeated often when telling parables. I hope that will be true of me. But apparently we can't please Him without this thing called FAITH.

If you read my first book, "The God Experiment," there is an attitude or expectation that I challenge us to embrace for the 12-week journey: an "all in" mindset. I've found in my walk with God, when I stretch my faith to the extreme, when I believe with all I am, and when I go full throttle, that is when growth happens most. That's when I discover new things about God and grow in my knowledge of Him, my understanding of His attributes, or who He says I am.

In the Faith Experiment, I want to challenge you once again to test each of these lessons on faith by taking them to the extreme and seeing how God will show up in your life as you do.

Another way of saying it is this: If you want to grow your faith, you're going to have to stretch your faith.

Let me tell you two stories. I imagine you can relate to at least one of them.

It was August of 2012, and our family had loaded into our 12-passenger van for the 30-hour drive out to Montana. My wife, Lisa, grew up in Montana. Her home was nestled in the canyon near the entrance to Glacier National Park. Beautiful mountain ranges are in every direction. Cascading waterfalls; catching a glimpse of an elusive bear, elk, or mountain goat; afternoons floating on the river; and riding four-wheelers along the cliff were the adventures that lay ahead. To say our kids were excited was an understatement. But before we got there, remember that 30-hour drive? Yeah, we had to tackle that first. Our family always splits it up into two long days of driving. Our one reprieve in the middle is a night at a hotel, which better have a pool where we can burn off some energy.

That night, after swimming for a couple of hours and relaxing, it was time to get ready for bed. As we were getting the kids ready one by one, a blood-curdling scream came from the other room. In runs our son Braden, holding his hand. Without getting into the gruesome details, Braden had accidentally slammed his finger in the door and nearly cut off the end of his finger. Let's just say, not a whole lot was holding the last inch of his finger in place.

I grabbed Braden and an older sibling for help, and headed to the closest hospital. When we arrived at the ER, the staff did a quick eval of the situation and created a game plan. The doctor looked at me and said, "We're going to do a quick X-ray just to see what's broken and then we'll know what to do next."

I asked him, "You think it's broken?"

"Based on what I'm looking at... for sure," he replied. He left to get the nurses and quickly put in the order for the X-ray.

While he stepped out, I took my son's good hand and I just started praying. All I'm thinking is a broken finger, maybe a torn ligament, who knows what else could be wrong, but this could really make this trip tough for Braden. So I prayed.

I don't know how to quantify the level of faith I had in that moment, but I remember praying like I was going to war for my son's finger. As I prayed for him, his hand started shaking. It seemed to make sense, I figured he was just really shaky due to the injury, similar to being in shock. The doctors and nurses wheeled him out of the room for the X-ray, assuring me it wouldn't take long. While they were out, I kept praying. My daughter who was with me started praying. I'm sure Lisa was praying. She had probably texted her dad who we were going to see, and I'm sure he was praying.

It didn't take long before Braden was back in the room to await the results of the X-ray. The doctor came walking in with a dumbfounded look on his face, and a statement I will never forget.

He said, "I don't know how this is possible, but nothing is broken. All we'll have to do is stitch up the finger and he should be good to go." And that's what happened. A few hours and some stitches later, we were on our way back to the hotel.

Now I know I'm not a doctor, but I looked at that injury pretty closely and I was sure it was broken. The nurses thought it was broken, the doctor who examined it thought it was broken. In the end, all I know is that he came home that night without a broken finger. Personally, I believe faith and our prayers made a real impact.

Second story. My wife periodically has migraine headaches. On one of those occasions I was watching her quietly suffer. And it is suffering. If you've dealt with a migraine before you know what it's like. You don't want to do anything other than shut your eyes and pray it away. The idea of cooking dinner, helping the kids with homework, cleaning up around the house, or doing your own work is miserable. Yet that's what Lisa was doing.

After watching her suffer through, I asked her, "Can I pray for your headache?" Of course she welcomed the prayer, so I prayed. And I prayed a good prayer, the type where you're pretty proud of what just came out of your mouth. It was a prayer that God should have been impressed with, for crying out loud... I was impressed by it. And it wasn't just because of the words, my heart was in it too.

When I finished praying, I asked her, "How do you feel?" Because after that angelic prayer, something should have happened. But, you guessed it, nothing did.

So why did faith work in one situation, but not in the other? Was there something that I needed to do differently? Is there a magic formula, or at the very least, a set of "best practices"?

This is the big question all of us wrestle with to some degree.

Jesus is even quoted as saying "you of little faith" about some individuals, or on another occasion He said, "I've never seen such great faith." In other words, He could see levels of faith. And the level of faith made a difference.

So for you and me, what can we do to grow our faith? Are there principles of faith that if applied will help our faith to be most effective? I believe there are "best practices" and principles we can learn that can grow our faith and make it most effective. That's what the Faith Experiment is all about. It's about taking our faith to new heights. It's about testing the limits, taking risks, and observing how God grows us in our faith.

I've been a Christian for 40 years, and a pastor for about 25 of those. One thing I know is that there is still so much growth for me in the area of my faith. So would you join me for just a short season of your life? Hop in on an experiment that will stretch us and grow us in our faith like we've never experienced before.

Let's dive in… Let's go "all in." Welcome to the Faith Experiment.

WEEK ONE

"…Truly I tell you, if you have faith as small as a mustard seed, you can say to this mountain, 'Move from here to there,' and it will move. Nothing will be impossible for you."

MATTHEW 17:20

Have you ever wondered why one person's faith seems to be more effective than another's? Have you ever felt like, "I can pray, but nothing is going to change," or maybe another time like, "I feel like my prayers are really making a difference"?

In Matthew 17, Jesus uses the imagery of a mustard seed and connects it to our faith. He describes what faith is capable of doing, that this thing called faith can move a mountain.

You may argue that Jesus wasn't being literal. Maybe he was, maybe he wasn't. I can't think of a whole lot of practical reasons for moving a mountain from one place to another. Whether it's literal or not, His point is clear. **Faith is meant to have the ability to move what seems immovable.** And not small moves. Jesus calls out the mountain because it is so massive. You've got this mind blowing statement that seems impossible, but is accurate.

Then, Jesus picks the mustard seed because it is one of the smallest seeds. I had a friend bring me some mustard seeds so I could see some firsthand. And Jesus is right… those seeds are tiny. And that's the point. There is something about faith that can be simple and small, yet incredibly effective.

So how do we grow our faith to be able to move and affect things like Jesus describes here?

What can we do to activate our faith and take it to a whole new level?

Before we go too far… to the individual who wouldn't claim to have faith at all, I'm thrilled you're willing to dive into a book on faith. If I could encourage you in any way, it would be in this way: explore these elements and principles, so if you choose to embrace faith, they will propel you faster into more profound expressions of faith.

What I truly believe God would say to all of us today is, "If you really knew what you could do even with your little faith, you'd be surprised."

And as He talks about faith the size of a tiny seed, I believe we have way too many inactive seeds.

Think about it, do you claim to be a Christ follower? When was the last time you were actively praying in faith for a mountain to move? Not a literal mountain, but a huge hurdle that stood before you. How many so-called "Christians" do you know? Are they prayer warriors? That is a term that we as Christians often ascribe to those who are serious about their faith and pray faith-filled mountain-moving-prayers.

What if that type of praying and that type of faith was not just for the elusive prayer warrior out there, but was for the everyday Christian out there? What if our problem as God's children is that we've got a whole bunch of inactive seeds in the family?

James 4:2b-3 says, "You do not have because you do not ask God. When you ask, you do not receive, because you ask with wrong motives, that you may spend what you get on your pleasures."

Many of us simply don't ask. And that's the problem. We are inactive seeds because we are members of the family of God, empowered with faith, yet not activating our faith. Perhaps we are afraid to ask because we have low expectations of His response to our request. Maybe we believe a lie that God has more important and greater concerns on His mind. Maybe we don't want to be disappointed if God doesn't answer our prayer the way we'd like. Whatever our reason, James is prodding us to ask.

He does, however, have a qualifier to our request. That qualifier is our motive. James says, "you do not receive, because you ask with wrong motives." So here is a good question to put over your request: does my prayer request align with the Kingdom of God? Does it align with God's heart?

Your motive cannot be revenge. Your motive cannot be coveting. Your motive cannot be anger. Your motive must be in line with His kingdom. And even with that, it doesn't mean it's a "gimme," but it does mean, ask away. Ask boldly, ask regularly, ask unashamedly... ASK.

What are some ways you can start today? What can you do to become an active seed?

Here's one simple thing I do. I pray for blessings over businesses in my community as I drive around. Especially for those I know are owned or led by Christan men and women. Why would I do that? Because Jeremiah 29:7 says "Also, seek the peace and prosperity of the city to which I have carried you into exile. Pray to the Lord for it, because if it prospers, you too will prosper."

It seems like praying for those in the cities to which we have been called is in line with the Kingdom of God. It's not a selfish request, nor a coveting based request, it's a kingdom request. So while I'm driving from one place to another, I might as well be an active seed, praying for mountains to move and blessings to come to these businesses.

If you're a teacher or a student, you could pray for peace over your classroom as you walk into that space. How many times have you walked into that space and just "got down to business"? For anyone in the marketplace, you could do the same thing in any work space. Perhaps you've missed the most important opportunity in your day as you've been an inactive seed.

As you walk into that important meeting later today, how about praying for God's favor to be over the meeting?

How about the big project you're working on? Instead of simply tackling the project, ask God for His wisdom over the project.

This is what it means to be an active seed. That our faith, like a seed, is planted and is actually producing fruit.

In the middle of the 2021-2022 NFL season I was watching a Sunday Night Football game. The Seahawks were playing the Steelers. Cris Collinsworth and Mike Tirico were calling the game. The game was nearing the end and Darrell Taylor of the Seahawks got injured. It's one of those injuries that you never want to see happen. It appeared to be a neck or back injury. He was lying on the field motionless for what seemed like an eternity. Both teams took a knee on the field. Multiple commercials played to fill the time. As time went by, Cris Collinsworth and Mike Tirico talked about how they felt watching this unfold. You could hear the concern in their voices and their heartfelt love for the players and their families. Cris then said, "If you're so inclined" and paused for a second. Probably wrestling through whether he could say what was going to come out of his mouth next on live TV, and then he went there. He said, "If you're so inclined… if you're a praying person, now's a good time to pray."

As soon as Cris said that, it hit me… I'M A PRAYING PERSON. How could it be that I had been watching this unfold for 10 minutes and it took the announcer to say, "If you're inclined to pray, now's a great time to pray" for me to realize this is what I should have been doing all along.

What's crazy is I'm the pastor of a church. I've been a Christian for 40 years. I would consider myself to be someone of strong faith. Yet there I was, an inactive seed.

How about you? What can you do today to activate your faith? Your faith doesn't have to be showy or impressive. In fact, Jesus seems to point to something much more simple and small. Just a small seed is all it takes.

DAILY CHALLENGE: Maybe the best place to start is to pray a heartfelt prayer like this: *God, would you grow my faith today? Help me to be an active seed. Help me to pray boldly and unashamedly for things that I know are on your heart.* Then keep your eyes open today and aim to pray in faith for at least three things that would be a step toward being an active seed. At the end of the day, write down what you prayed for. Why did you pray for those things? What were your motives? Did you sense anything happening in your faith today as you prayed?

NOTES

"Then he said to them all: 'Whoever wants to be my disciple must deny themselves and take up their cross daily and follow me.'"

LUKE 9:23

It's Sunday morning. I've been at the church since a little before 7 a.m. I've run through my message one final time before I preach it. Our worship team and tech team have been rehearsing and they sound amazing. I've done my quick rounds through the foyer, shaken as many hands as I can and answered a few final questions from some team members. We've prayed backstage and the first service is just getting started. I stand alone backstage and it hits me in the chest like a ton of bricks, just like it does every Sunday. I see things as clear as day. **All this effort, all this prep, all we do is for nothing if God doesn't show up and touch people's lives.**

By now, as a team we've already prayed, our prayer and care teams have been praying through the building and for our services. Probably tons of people have been praying.

But this moment is an important moment for me personally each Sunday. It's the moment when I pray a different prayer. It's the moment I personally surrender all this to Him.

I surrender the next few hours to Him, I surrender my mouth, I surrender my thoughts, I surrender my notes and my intentions, I surrender my plans and my hopes, I surrender every person in the building and every person watching online to Him… I surrender it all.

And in the process of surrender I also lay down every burden that I've wrongfully placed upon myself. I lay down any personal expectations I've created in my mind and all the eternal outcomes. They are in His hands and I'm relying on Him for everything. In this moment, what often feels like the weight of the world is lifted off my shoulders and placed on

His. And I walk onto the stage carrying no extra weight, with my goal of serving just ONE: Him alone. And everything else seems to fade away.

That's just one way surrender looks for me on Sunday mornings.

This week we are going to focus on surrender in regard to how it interacts with our faith. I believe surrender is at the center of growing our faith.

When Jesus was teaching He said this:

"Then he said to them all: 'Whoever wants to be my disciple must deny themselves and take up their cross daily and follow me.'"
LUKE 9:23

Often we think that being a Jesus follower or Christian simply starts by choosing to follow Him. It does start that way, but it's more than that. It's more than just following, it's surrender.

A surrender of what?

Look at the whole passage, but especially this part: "take up their cross daily and follow me."

Now, we don't have death sentences by crucifixion anymore; thank goodness. But this statement was a declaration of death to yourself. In Jesus' day if you saw someone carrying their cross, they were carrying it to their own crucifixion. It was their walk of shame, the last walk they would ever take. It was for those whose lives had already been kissed goodbye.

Jesus' point is not to say that your life doesn't matter. But following Jesus requires a level of surrender of your life. It's a surrender of your own will. It's a surrender of your own ways. It's a surrender of your control. It's a surrender of your dreams. This is what surrendering your life looks like.

When you effectively surrender everything, you'll realize that the world cannot take anything from you that you've already willingly given to Him.

Another way of saying it is: you can't lose what you've already given away.

This is why on a Sunday morning, I can't lose in terms of the results in people's lives, when I already surrendered the results to Him. I can't lose in terms of my expectations, because I surrendered my expectations to Him. I can't lose in terms of how many people showed up or how they responded, because I surrendered all the people to Him.

But this process of surrender is not just for Sundays, and it's not just for pastors. Jesus says, "take up their cross DAILY and follow me."

Meaning, this thing called surrender is not a one and done thing. Instead it's a daily thing. It's a Monday, Tuesday, Wednesday, Thursday, Friday, Saturday, Sunday thing. It's an everyday practice that continually propels your faith forward. It's also a daily practice, because if you're like me, the thing that you surrendered control of yesterday, you try to control again today. And you have to remind your heart that you're choosing to surrender that area of your life to Christ once again.

Maybe you've experienced it like this. You've got a big financial hurdle in front of you. You surrender it to the Lord. You feel a sense of peace and calm come over your heart, even a sense of courage and security and faith that God will provide. Then the next day you wake up and fear has captured your heart once again and you find yourself worried about how you will tackle this financial hurdle. And once again, you'll find that the most important thing you do is surrender today that which you successfully surrendered yesterday.

You may need to surrender daily:
- your spouse
- your child
- your relationship status
- your relationship with your boss or coworkers
- your finances
- your grades at school or your success at work
- the promotion you desire
- the house you want
- the health need you have
- the emotional desires you have
- and the list could go on and on… it's everything that is a part of your life.

That's why Jesus said, "take up their cross daily," in other words, surrender all the aspects of your life daily, and follow after Him.

DAILY CHALLENGE: What do you like to control? What is the heavy weight that you feel rests upon your shoulders? Let's activate our faith through the simple step of surrender. But maybe the most important aspect of surrender is to practice it early and often. Create a list of things that could be helpful for you to surrender to Him daily. Now take some time to simply pray the following prayer over each item on your list, "God I surrender _____ to you."

NOTES

RECKLESS SURRENDER

"Trust in the LORD with all your heart
  and lean not on your own understanding;
  in all your ways submit to him,
  and he will make your paths straight."

PROVERBS 3:5-6

I've only jumped out of a plane once. Yes, it was on purpose; yes, I was skydiving; yes, I was attached to someone and yes, it was on my bucket list. I remember that morning pretty clearly. There was a chill in the air and the skies were clear. It was early July and a few friends and I were getting ready to do something none of us had ever done before. We arrived and the instructors sat us down. They talked through some simple safety protocols, told us a little bit about what to expect, had us sign our lives away and then simply stated (stated, not asked) "Let's go!"

As we were walking out to the plane, I asked the instructor, "What about landing and coming in? You didn't cover that earlier."

To which he replied, "I'll tell you on the way down."

"ON THE WAY DOWN."

Are you kidding me? ON THE WAY DOWN. If you're like me, you're thinking, "Isn't that a little too late to cover the landing part?"

I felt way underprepared, unequipped, uninformed, and completely reckless. I think I rationalized it by thinking, "Well, we are jumping out of a plane and the whole concept is kinda reckless, so I guess the recklessness of the whole process is to not have a clue what you're doing and just go for it, RIGHT?"

I don't remember entirely what I was thinking, but I do remember thinking, "Even though I have no idea what to do, I'm going to have to trust the instructor that I'm attached to."

And that's what I did. I put my life in the hands of a little man probably six inches shorter than me, and weighing at least 50 pounds less than me. I trusted that he knew what he was doing and could take care of my life as we jumped out of that plane together.

And that's what we did.
And it was exhilarating.
And yes, on the way down he gave me two sentences of instructions on how to land and it was more than sufficient for what I needed to land safely.

To say I had to trust him in what felt pretty reckless was an understatement. But in our walks with God we will often feel the same way.

You may feel pretty reckless at times.

Over the next three days we're going to work our way through Proverbs 3:5-6. It begins by saying, "Trust in the Lord with all your heart and lean not on your own understanding;"

The word TRUST means to have confidence in, to be secure in, to feel safe in, or even be careless.

I think that's how you'll sometimes feel in this thing called faith. You might feel a little careless or a little reckless. You might just feel like you're jumping out of a plane, strapped to God, but feeling way unprepared and a bit reckless. Trusting Jesus and how I follow Him might seem a little reckless at times. Sometimes it will seem reckless to me, and sometimes it will seem reckless to others.

The sooner you recognize that surrender to God and "trusting" God will sometimes feel reckless, the better you'll be. Not because it makes jumping out of the plane with Jesus easier, it just helps it make a little more sense. Or at least it normalizes the process.

It's like how people will tell you, "You're never quite ready to start your first job… own your own home… have your first child… **and that's all** normal." It's in all these firsts that people say, "You can't fully prep for it, you won't be fully ready for it, but you'll be okay as you hop into it—**that's normal.**"

I wish someone would have told me early in my faith, **"Truly following Jesus will feel and look reckless at times, and that's normal."**

So I'm telling you now, the act of faith in surrender will often feel reckless and that's normal. God may even lead you on what feels like a reckless journey. But as you surrender daily to Him, He will make sense of the apparent reckless journey that you're on and take you on a great adventure. It will be as thrilling as jumping out of a plane... maybe more. So here we go: jumping into reckless surrender with Him.

DAILY CHALLENGE: What does reckless faith mean to you? Does that seem foolish? Where in your life do you feel like trusting Him feels scary and reckless right now? Is there an area in your life that is hard to surrender to God because you don't have all the details worked out? What do you need to surrender to Him today?

NOTES

....

....

....

....

....

....

....

"Trust in the LORD with all your heart
   and lean not on your own understanding;
   in all your ways submit to him,
   and he will make your paths straight."

PROVERBS 3:5-6

Yesterday we talked about how faith and surrender will sometimes feel reckless. It may feel like you're jumping out of a plane strapped to God with little understanding of where you're going or how you'll land. But you're taking the leap of faith all the same.

What often goes hand in hand with feeling reckless in your surrender is the next phrase in Proverbs 3:5, which says, *"lean not on your own understanding."*

To "lean not on your own understanding" means that at some point, to embrace this thing called faith, you will have to forgo being able to have every question answered. You will have to surrender to not knowing the outcome. Faith is actually believing in what we do not see, and cannot comprehend. **We cannot logic or reason our way through every aspect of that which is divine or supernatural.**

We call it supernatural, because that's what it is. It is beyond what seems natural. To lean on our own understanding is to make sense of what seems natural. So to lean NOT on my own understanding is to forgo my expectation to be able to reason my way through my situation.

Leaning not on your own understanding is literally the leap of faith. It may not make sense, I don't have all my questions answered, it doesn't seem logical or always reasonable, but I'm trusting God all the same.

My wife, Lisa, and I have nine kids. That was never our plan. We both came from families with three siblings, so that seemed like a logical number for us when we started talking about having a family. Maybe we could have four kids, but that would be our "crazy number." Well, the Lord had other plans for us. We started with twins and then a third a few years later. And then we were at that place, wondering if we would have any more. And just when Lisa and I started to "wonder" if we should consider having more kids, it seemed like the Lord took our "wondering" off the table, because we found out we were having our fourth. After our fourth, we started "wondering" if we were completely done, and in the middle of our "wondering" we found out we were pregnant with our fifth. If you think "wondering" is code for sex, you're wrong. We were genuinely wondering what God had for us. Well, continuing on, after the fifth arrived our "wondering" was completely over at that point and we knew we were done. That's when we found out we were pregnant with our sixth.

At this point, it almost seemed comical and also somewhat embarrassing that we seemed to stink at family planning. There was nothing logical in what was happening. (Yes, we know how it happens.) But God seemed to be defying our plans and our strategies. It didn't make sense, it didn't seem wise, and in some ways it defied our logical understanding. It took us till our sixth child for Lisa and I to really start praying, "God help us to see kids as you see kids." Of course we loved each and every one of our kids. We couldn't imagine life without each of them. But it still hadn't been our plan.

As we processed with the Lord and read scripture about children, we seemed to always find the same thing. Kids are always a blessing in scripture. Kids are always a gift from the Lord. Having kids is always good. So our question shifted. It shifted from "How many kids do we want to have?" to "How many blessings does the Lord want to give us in this area of kids?"

For Lisa and I, we felt like the Lord impressed on our hearts to have nine. So that's why we have nine. We're not pro "large families", we are pro "being obedient to God." For some that may be having one child, two children, three or more. It may be having none. It may be adopting or fostering kids.

You probably have a logical plan that makes perfect sense and you understand it. And all I know is that God probably has a better plan that's less logical, doesn't make sense, and is hard to understand. And that is just part of our journey of surrender.

DAILY CHALLENGE: What area in your life is difficult to surrender to God because you don't have complete understanding around it? Is there a question that you've wished God would answer? Can you surrender and lean not on your own understanding? This may mean forgoing the right to have all your questions answered before you trust Him. While you may not be able to understand everything God is doing in your situation, is it possible He still has a good plan that you can surrender to today?

NOTES

"Trust in the LORD with all your heart
  and lean not on your own understanding;
  in all your ways submit to him,
  and he will make your paths straight."

PROVERBS 3:5-6

I've always been pretty good with my money. Even at a young age, as soon as I could push a lawn mower, I went to my neighbors to try to earn some money mowing lawns. And that's what I did until I was 12 and could officially work at the local golf course as a caddie. Then from there other jobs came and went, but I was always making some money and handling it wisely. I was frugal and did my best not to overspend. I saved, I balanced my checkbook, I tithed (that's giving 10% to the church) and I knew where almost every dollar went.

In short, I like handling my money, I like having enough of it (who doesn't?) and I like feeling like I'm in control of it. So it was definitely a leap of faith and a huge stretch for me the first time I felt like God called Lisa and I into extravagant generosity.

It was one area of my life that I always loved to control and now we felt like God was asking us to surrender it to Him. We had learned to surrender the number of kids we would have to Him. Why our money too? In some ways I was thinking, "Let me stay in control of my money since it seems like we're out of control in this area of having kids." Or, "Let me stay in control here (with money), so I can afford to handle where we're out of control over there (with kids)."

But God doesn't want portions of your life. He wants all of it. Not because He's a power-hungry control-freak of a God, but because He has a good plan for you in every area of your life. Surrender just happens to be the path to that good plan for you and me.

Which is why as we continue working our way through Proverbs 3:5-6 it goes on to say, "in all your ways submit to Him". Did you see it? ALL your ways. Not some of your ways, not some of the areas of your life where you're not a control freak, not some of the areas where you feel comfortable surrendering, but ALL of your ways.

The Hebrew word that gets translated as "your ways" can also be translated as manner, habit, way, or journey.

So in every area of our lives, including our habits, our manners, and every place our journey might take us, we need to learn to surrender to Him.

In fact, that word that gets translated as "submit" can also be translated as "surrender."

So we can read it this way: "In all your ways surrender to Him."

I know we have already practiced this prayer this week, but one of the most simple ways I pray is, "God I surrender…"

I just work my way through everything in my life. My spouse, my kids, my work, my finances, my dreams, my worries, my questions, my longings–all of it I simply surrender to Him.

In doing so, I'm also setting myself up for something. I'm setting myself up for God to produce His kingdom fruit in it.

Remember how we started this week using the picture of a mustard seed? We talked about what it could look like for each of us to be effective seeds. We all know seeds ultimately grow to produce fruit. As I surrender everything to Him, I'm actually setting everything up for the greatest fruit to be produced in it.

Conversely, as long as it's in my control, I actually restrain its full kingdom potential.

Back to my money. When Lisa and I felt like the Lord was calling us to give an extravagant gift to our church, we were scared to death to step into that level of giving. It was beyond our bank account balance, it was beyond our budget, it was definitely beyond what seemed logical. But it was what we sensed God was calling us to do. So we did it, and God provided in such a way that we could give the gift and then He provided for us in ways beyond what we could ask or imagine after having given it.

Lisa and I now have dozens and dozens of God stories of financial provision and blessing in our lives. The amazing thing is if we had chosen to remain in control of our finances and not surrender them to God we would have missed out on the countless blessings and provisions that we've seen Him provide over the years. We would have restrained God's kingdom potential from being displayed in that area of our lives.

The verse ends by saying, "and he will make your paths straight."

Surrendering to Him may seem reckless at times. It may seem illogical at times and beyond human understanding. It may seem like God is calling you to surrender the one area that is so difficult to turn over to Him. But I've seen His faithfulness over and over again in my life and that last line in verse 6 may best describe what it feels like. It feels like the path is suddenly straight.

It's like the path where you are to walk is incredibly obvious to you. You can't imagine taking a different step in a different direction. Like when we gave that extravagant gift, we couldn't imagine doing anything else. It was the most obvious step for us to take in our journey. In fact, there seemed to be no other step before us to take other than giving that gift.

And that's how it will be for you as well. As you surrender all these different areas of your life to Him, He will direct your path in such a way that there will seem to be no other way. It will be the best path and it will be good.

DAILY CHALLENGE: What's one area in your life that you like to control? Why is it scary to surrender? How could you take a step toward surrender in that area today?

FOR THE SPIRITUAL SEEKER: Maybe you'd call yourself a seeker, or someone testing this thing called faith. Perhaps after this week, working through aspects of surrender, you've been taking small steps in surrendering things to God. Maybe you're coming to the place where you're starting to "believe." Maybe you're coming to the place where you'd like to fully surrender everything to Him today. If not today, maybe later in this journey. Just mark this page as a place you may want to come back to. But if full surrender to God is something you know is your next step, the following prayer is a simple way to trust Jesus as your Lord and Savior.

Dear Lord Jesus, I know that I am a sinner, and I ask for Your forgiveness. I believe You died for my sins and rose from the dead. I turn from my sins and invite You to come into my heart and life. I want to surrender everything to you. I want to trust and follow You as my Lord and Savior.

NOTES

"May these words of my mouth and this meditation of my heart
    be pleasing in your sight,
    LORD, my Rock and my Redeemer."

PSALMS 19:14

"so is my word that goes out from my mouth:
    It will not return to me empty,
    but will accomplish what I desire
    and achieve the purpose for which I sent it."

ISAIAH 55:11

There is something profound in letting a verse or truth from God simmer in your soul. This is real Biblical meditation. Sometimes when we think of meditation we think of the practice of meditation in eastern religions, which is often the emptying of your mind. Biblical meditation is the complete opposite. It is the filling of your mind and the purposeful "rethinking" of a good or true thought.

Over the next two days, write down an idea, verse, or concept that you want to think (or rethink) about. What do you want to let your soul simmer in for a bit longer?

What idea was most challenging this week?

What day or concept do you want to rethink about?

....

....

....

....

....

NOTES

....

....

....

....

....

....

....

....

....

WEEK TWO

WEEK TWO / DAY ONE

PURITY:
IS HE LISTENING?

¹⁰ "For,

'Whoever would love life

and see good days

must keep their tongue from evil

and their lips from deceitful speech.

¹¹ They must turn from evil and do good;

they must seek peace and pursue it.

¹² For the eyes of the Lord are on the righteous

and his ears are attentive to their prayer,

but the face of the Lord is against those who do evil.'"

I PETER 3:10-12

Has something like this happened to you before? I walked into the house after a day of work and Lisa looked at me and asked, "Did you get my text?"

I replied, "No, what text?"

She said, "I needed you to pick up hamburger buns on your way home."

As I pulled out my phone from my pocket, it dinged, indicating I had a new text message. I looked at it and sure enough, it was from my wife. And I smiled sadly and said, "It just came through… Sorry."

I'm sure you've experienced something like that in your life. You're trying to get a message to someone and for whatever reason it's just lost out there in cyberspace. I recently replied to a message from a friend that seemed pretty time-sensitive and pretty serious. They were asking for prayer for a family member who was in crisis. Shortly after I replied to them, they responded by saying that message had been sent over a year ago. WOW, talk about a message being blocked or lost in cyberspace–that one takes the win.

There is nothing more frustrating in communication than trying to communicate and the message not getting through.

What if the same thing can actually happen in prayer? What if the same thing can happen to prayers we prayed that we thought were full-of-faith-prayers? Is it possible for our prayers to not make it through to the One (our Heavenly Father) we are praying to?

Consider the following verses:

"...his [God's] ears are attentive to their prayer,
but the face of the Lord is against those..."

1 PETER 3:12

"When you ask, you do not receive..."

JAMES 4:3

"When you spread out your hands in prayer,
I [God] hide my eyes from you;
even when you offer many prayers,
I am not listening. ..."

ISAIAH 1:15

These are humbling, eye-opening and sobering verses. In each one we see God not listening, not responding to, or even hiding His eyes from His people.

I've said it this way before. **Every prayer you pray is heard, but not every prayer you pray is listened to.**

Picture it like this. Let's imagine my family is finishing up dinner. After the meal, our kids are each assigned a kitchen chore they need to do before they leave the kitchen. This night, instead of diligently completing the chore, they notice the beautiful weather outside and hear their friends playing at the park nearby. Before Lisa or I notice, they have run outside to the park. With a bit of frustration, I get up from the table and start doing their chores. Lisa and I work together and knock out the kids' chores in a short time. An hour goes by and the kids return home from the park. They walk into the kitchen and ask, "Can we have ice cream with all the toppings?" And they start pulling out more dishes and all the fixings to go on their ice cream.

But we reply, "No, you cannot have ice cream." To which they start to repeatedly beg to have some. We remind them of our family rules and point out to them how they abandoned us and their responsibilities. They continue to beg. But Lisa and I hold our ground because they need to learn a lesson here. They beg and beg and beg. I look at them and say, "Stop asking. I hear you, but I am not listening to this request any longer."

I imagine God looks at us (His children) at times and is thinking the same thing. I HEAR YOU, BUT I AM NOT LISTENING.

What would cause God not to listen to our prayers?

Isaiah 1:15 states it the most bluntly. "Even when you offer many prayers, I am not listening."

There is something happening in the context here that is causing their prayers to not be listened to.

This may seem obvious, but faith is not effective if it is not being listened to. You can pray the most faith-filled prayer, the most eloquent prayer, the most Biblically true prayer, but if it is not being listened to, it is not effective.

If we want our faith to move mountains, then we ought to be aware of the things we can do to set up our prayers to be effective or not effective.

So what's happening in the context of Isaiah that is causing God not to listen to their prayers?

Let's check out a little bit more of the passage.

15 "When you spread out your hands in prayer,
 I [God] hide my eyes from you;
 even when you offer many prayers,
 I am not listening.

Your hands are full of blood!
¹⁶ Wash and make yourselves clean.
  Take your evil deeds out of my sight;
  stop doing wrong."

ISAIAH 1:15-16

The reason God is not listening to their prayers is because their lives are consumed with evil. Sin and its deceitfulness has corrupted them as the people of God. They may be going to church, they may look like they are worshiping, they may be praying, but their wickedness all week long has blocked the effectiveness of their faith.

This week we are going to consider something crucial to effective faith: PURITY. We will see how purity actually propels our faith forward with great efficiency. While conversely, the opposite (sin/ wickedness/ deceit) can actually block the effectiveness of our faith. It can block our prayers from being listened to.

Listen to how 1 Peter 3:12 captures this idea.

"'For the eyes of the Lord are on the righteous
  and his ears are attentive to their prayer,
  but the face of the Lord is against those who do evil.'"

I PETER 3:12

Do you see both of God's responses? His ears are attentive to the righteous, but He is against those who do evil.

This week we are going to focus on principles that can set us up to live in purity. And purity sets up our faith to be the most effective it can be.

But for today, consider this. Are your faith-filled prayers being heard? Or, do you have ongoing sin in your life? I'm not talking about if you still sin. Of course you do, we all do. I'm talking about blatant, purposeful, choosing-to-continue-to-live-in-sin lifestyles.

It may be the sinful romantic relationship you continue to stay in. It may be the ongoing lying you continue to live in. It may be the addiction you continue to foster. It may be the anger you continue to ignore. It may be the trash you continue to watch or listen to. The point is, it's the things that you willingly CONTINUE to have as a part of your life.

It's one thing to confess (which is simply to declare) your sin to God, with the full intention of returning to it again tomorrow. It's another thing to repent (which means to turn away) from your sins and desire to not go back to it. This is where we take practical steps that lead you toward freedom from your sin.

It is not confession, but repentance that will make your faith effective.

DAILY CHALLENGE: After today's reading, do you think your faith-filled prayers are effective and being listened to? When it comes to sin, do you confess or do you repent of your sin? What steps do you need to take today to lead you toward freedom from your sin? Is there someone you need to share your struggle with? Consider sharing whatever has you ensnared with a trusted Christian friend. Join a nearby Celebrate Recovery group or a Small Group in your church. But let's take some bold steps toward freedom today!

NOTES

WEEK TWO / DAY TWO

PURITY:
CHOOSE TO DISTANCE
YOURSELF FROM THE WORLD

³ "When you ask, you do not receive, because you ask with wrong motives, that you may spend what you get on your pleasures.
⁴ You adulterous people, don't you know that friendship with the world means enmity against God? Therefore, anyone who chooses to be a friend of the world becomes an enemy of God."

JAMES 4:3-4

I remember when I was younger, SNL ("Saturday Night Live") was cleaner in content and was legitimately funny. It was one of the few shows that I longed to stay up to watch and catch the new sketches of the week. Part of the reason was there was no YouTube or place where you could watch the show immediately afterward. If you missed it, you missed it. And if you missed it, you would be in the dark the next day when everyone talked about their favorite sketches and tried their best to quote them. It was a clear instance of FOMO (Fear Of Missing Out).

There has always been a draw to wanting to fit in with the world. We naturally want to belong "with" the whole, whoever the whole is.

Yesterday we talked about something that blocks effective faith: sin. James 4:3 leans into this concept of prayers not being answered. But there is a reason for it. In verse 4, James makes an observation of what blocks our prayers.

He says *"anyone who chooses to be a friend of the world becomes an enemy of God."*

The thing that blocks our prayers is our friendship with the world. Conversely, distancing ourselves from the norms of this world helps set us up for lives of purity and effective faith.

Now, when he uses the word "world," he's not telling us to be unfriendly to people in the world. That's not it at all. He's saying that you can't love the things of this world, the perspectives of this world, the value system of this world, and love God. They are at odds with each other.

You belong to His world and His kingdom, not this world and this kingdom.

Your faith will rise as you purposefully choose which kingdom you're going to belong to and which kingdom you're going to be close to.

A simple prayer that I think propels us toward purity is this: "I don't belong to this world. I don't belong to this kingdom. I belong to His world, I belong to His kingdom. The things of this world will not distract or attract my heart away from His kingdom."

When it comes to purity, our God is holy. And holy means set apart. He is set apart from everything in this world. He is entirely pure and entirely holy.

What is amazing is we have a unique opportunity while we live. While we are alive on this earth, we operate within two realms simultaneously.

Ephesians 2 says,

[4] "But because of his great love for us, God, who is rich in mercy, [5] made us alive with Christ even when we were dead in transgressions—it is by grace you have been saved. [6] And God raised us up with Christ and seated us with him in the heavenly realms in Christ Jesus,"

EPHESIANS 2:4-6

Do you see it? It says we are seated with Christ in the heavenly realms.

Most of you feel like life is very much here. And that's true. Physically, you are here. However, spiritually you have access to His kingdom there.

What does your position of being seated with Christ in the heavenly realms (and having access to His Kingdom there) get you here and now?

I want to highlight three things: your spiritual authority, power, and inheritance.

Let me just make a brief statement about each.

Authority- This is the reality that "greater is He [the Holy Spirit] who is in you, than he [Satan] who is in the world." (1 John 4:4, NASB) Because of the ruling Holy Spirit in the life of Christ followers, we actually have authority over the works of the enemy.

Power- This is the ability to see the strength of God displayed through our earthly shells, that we call our bodies. That power and that strength are lots of different things. It's courage in the midst of the storms of life, it's healing over sickness, it's perseverance in the trials, etc.

It is what the Apostle Paul was referring to when he said, "for when I am weak, then I am strong" (2 Corinthians 12:10, NIV).

Inheritance- This is all the resources of heaven. The resources of heaven touch everything from our finances to our physical bodies to our emotional needs.

The point is, there is a ton from His world that we have access to here and now. But here's the reality, and it may be a gut check for you. You and I **can't** physically be here, but spiritually rule from there, with sin prevalent in our lives.

The reason why is because God is Holy. And I can't operate out of a Holy place and Holy Kingdom with sin prevalent in me. That which is prevalent in me (sin) cannot be there (in heaven).

Meanwhile, the opposite is true. Purity sets me up to physically be here, but spiritually operate from there. Spiritually I can unashamedly go to His throne of grace and access all that is in His Kingdom.

We have to ask ourselves, are we most concerned about FOMO and as a result we love the things of this world? Or, are we setting ourselves up to operate from His Kingdom?

DAILY CHALLENGE: Does FOMO draw you into things of this world? Are there things from this world that you love to hold onto, that you know God is opposed to? Make a list of anything that you think you should distance yourself from. Then pray this prayer, *"I don't belong to this world. I don't belong to this kingdom. I belong to His world, I belong to His kingdom. The things of this world will not distract or attract my heart away from His kingdom."*

NOTES

WEEK TWO / DAY THREE

PURITY:
CHOOSE HUMILITY

⁶ "But he gives us more grace. That is why Scripture says:
  'God opposes the proud
  but shows favor to the humble.'
⁷ Submit yourselves, then, to God. ..."

JAMES 4:6-7

As I write this, the Russian-Ukrainian war is entering its 27th day. It's been horrific to watch it unfold. My heart breaks for the injustice and unwarranted bloodshed that is occurring. I just saw a news clip where the reporter referred to Putin as a proud man.

What does that mean... a "proud" man?

It doesn't mean that he should be proud of what he's accomplished or that this is a proud moment in the life of Russia. Instead, the reporter is referring to the condition of Putin's heart. And we all instinctively know that this pride is an unhealthy, toxic and isolating pride.

Today we want to continue to press into purity so that our prayers will be heard and our faith will be effective. As we continue in the next verses in our passage in James, he says, "God opposes the proud but shows favor to the humble."

That verse states it pretty clearly. God opposes the proud. Perhaps we could go as far as to say God is not listening to the prayers of those whose hearts are filled with pride. Then James goes on to say that God "shows favor to the humble."

The next principle that propels us toward purity and toward effective faith is to **Choose Humility.**

Let's first break down what pride is.

We often think of pride as simply being super proud of yourself or your accomplishments. We may think of it as thinking highly of yourself. But pride is not just thinking of yourself as "so great."

Pride is most often a false sense of security in yourself.

It's thinking you're above others, or above the rules. It's thinking you're untouchable. It's the attitude that I'm going to live my life however I want to live it, and I carry a mindset that I really don't think anything can take me down. That is pride.

1 Corinthians 10:12-13 says, "[12] So, if you think you are standing firm, be careful that you don't fall! [13] No temptation has overtaken you except what is common to mankind. And God is faithful; he will not let you be tempted beyond what you can bear. But when you are tempted, He will also provide a way out so that you can endure it."

I memorized that verse a long time ago this way: "let him who thinks he stands take heed lest he fall." (New King James Version.)

In other words, if you think you're untouchable, if you think you're "all that", be careful: this is your warning before you fall. You've probably heard the saying, "Pride comes before the fall."

The key to standing up under temptation is humility. Notice what verse 13 points to. GOD is faithful... HE will not let you be tempted beyond... HE will also provide an escape.

Temptation will come your way, and if you're relying on yourself you will fall. If you are humble and rely on God, you can overcome it.

Humility propels us toward trusting God in all things and in turn propels us toward purity, and as I stated on Day 1 of this week, "Purity sets up our faith to be the most effective it can be."

So choose humility.

DAILY CHALLENGE: Maybe you haven't thought of pride as being a problem in your life. But ask yourself, do you have a false sense of security in yourself? Do you live your life according to your own standards, by your own rules? Ask God to reveal to you if there are any places in your life where pride has taken root. What would it look like for you to humble yourself today?

NOTES

WEEK TWO / DAY FOUR

PURITY:
CHOOSE YOUR ESCAPE ROUTE

"...Resist the devil, and he will flee from you."

JAMES 4:7

Do you remember doing fire drills growing up? I used to love fire drills simply because it was a 10-15 minute break randomly in the middle of the school day. I'm sure we were doing something important, but for me it was just about getting fresh air and seeing my friends for a brief moment. The best were the days when a squirrel would get into the transformer on the electric pole next to the school and fry it out. For whatever reason, the fire alarm would go off and the school would lose power. These occurrences would usually mean students spent over an hour outside while the fire trucks came and the electric company reset the transformer. It was a sad day for the squirrel, but a great day for every kid in school who unexpectedly got an extra hour of recess.

While I might have had other things on my mind during these drills, I know what we were really doing was rehearsing our fastest and most effective escape routes from potential danger.

This same principle is also one of the most effective things you and I can do to help us live a life of purity.

And that is, **Choose Your Predetermined Response To Temptation.**

As we continue in our passage this week in James 4, verse 7 goes on to say, "Resist the devil, and he will flee from you."

This is the purposeful pushing back against the schemes of the devil in your life. The reality is the devil is not that creative. He doesn't tempt you in a creative new way every day. Instead, temptation often comes in similar patterns. And because it comes in common patterns, we can prepare with predetermined escape routes for the temptation.

Just like rehearsing for a fire drill so you can escape the danger quickly, we need to rehearse our escape route from the temptations that the enemy will put in front of us.

If you just hope to win when the devil tempts you, you will probably fail. But if you rehearse in your mind how to say no, walk away, do what is right, etc., your predetermined choice will push back against temptation when it comes your way. That predetermined choice will set you up for purity.

I was a youth pastor for over a decade. During those years, I can't tell you the number of times I had students come to me and confess the temptation they had placed themselves in, and it always went like this: "We were alone in my basement watching a movie…"

It was always that: "alone in a basement watching a movie." I heard it so many times, I eventually just started telling teen couples outright, "Don't go watch a movie alone in a basement… EVER!"

I know it sounds a little legalistic and a bit dogmatic, but I knew how their story would play out if they put themselves in the common path of temptation.

It's exactly like the verse that we read yesterday.

"No temptation has overtaken you except what is common to mankind. …"
1 CORINTHIANS 10:13

There is nothing new in the temptation that is coming your way. Many others have faced it before in the exact same way that you will face it now. The Apostle Paul continues in verse 13, "… But when you are tempted, he will also provide a way out so that you can endure it."
Yes, there is an escape route available to you. You just need to know it and rehearse it.

Funny enough, after I started giving teen couples that advice, I heard far fewer confession stories with that beginning. It's because they knew their escape route would keep them from temptation.

How about you? What is your common pattern toward sin? You likely take the same route to it every time. What could your predetermined escape route be to the most common temptations that come against you?

One of the pastors on staff here at Lakeland has a creative escape route they have rehearsed in their home. They even have a key word they say to remind them. Any time there is something inappropriate on TV, they say "microwave" and everyone looks over at the microwave in the kitchen until the inappropriate content is gone. It's a simple, yet effective, predetermined escape route for temptation.

In doing all this, we are creating a path toward purity which sets us up to be children of God with effective faith.

DAILY CHALLENGE: None of us likes falling to the same sin or temptation time and time again. So today is the day to change all that. Instead of just hoping to beat the temptation next time it comes our way, let's create a plan today. Let's create an escape route and rehearse it in our minds. If you're able, tell someone the common temptation that comes your way and your intended escape route. Ask them to hold you accountable and ask you later how the escape route worked (or didn't work).

NOTES

WEEK TWO / DAY FIVE

PURITY:
CHOOSE TO PURSUE GOD

"Come near to God and he will come near to you. Wash your hands, you sinners, and purify your hearts, you double-minded."

JAMES 4:8

Have you ever had a person in your life, that the more you hang out with them, the more you like the person you become? You feel like you become a better individual, and you might be happier, more energized, simply as a result of being with them. I have a pastor friend of mine who is that way. Every time I am with this guy, I feel encouraged and uplifted and in turn I want to be a more encouraging and uplifting friend to those I interact with.

This final principle of the week that will lead us toward greater purity is to **Pursue God.**

In the same way that hanging out with certain individuals might help you become more like them, the same is true with God. The more you pursue Him and the closer you stay to Him, the more He (as the pure and Holy one) will rub off on you. His purity becomes our natural standard of purity.

The outcome of being in His presence is always purity.

We see this in the encounter of Isaiah coming into the throne room of God. As soon as he finds himself in the presence of God, his very first response is "... 'I am ruined! For I am a man of unclean lips,'" (Isaiah 6:5). He is immediately aware of his sin and his need for it to be done away with. He's fully aware that purity is the only way for him to remain in the presence of God. And that's what God does. He makes a way for Isaiah's sin to be cleansed so he can remain in God's presence.

The impact of the simple pursuit of God in your life will be profound. As James 4:8 says, "Come near to God and he will come near to you."

Drawing near to Him always brings conviction of sin wherever it is present in our lives and leads us to purity.

What could this look like for you today? What does it look like to draw near to God or to pursue God?

For me one of the ways I pursue Him is simply worshiping Him. Now before you think I'm just this super-spiritual guy who is on my knees worshiping God before the sun rises each day, it really never looks that way. I'm a multitasker and what I often will do is worship while I work out. It is usually in the form of watching worship videos on YouTube while I'm lifting weights. Right there, while sitting on my bench in between sets, I'll be worshiping with the music. Sometimes I sing along, but honestly that's pretty rare. Sometimes I'm just humming along. Sometimes I'll raise my hands while I worship. And sometimes I just sit there quietly and agree in my heart with all that is being sung. But the point is I'm pursuing Him. And in that pursuit I find what I'm looking for. I find Him, I enter His presence. And inevitably, God regularly brings things to my mind that need to be confessed and repented of. Why? Because you can't stay in His presence without purity as an outcome. And as I pursue Him, He graciously restores me, teaches me, encourages me and gives me what I need.

You can pursue Him during your drive time into work. You can pursue Him during a daily walk. You can pursue Him while you enjoy your first cup of coffee in the morning. However you prioritize it is up to you. But prioritize your pursuit, and purity will be a natural outcome.

DAILY CHALLENGE: When in your past have you had sweet moments in the presence of God? Where were you? What were you doing? If it was in a worship setting, you may want to listen to worship music as you pursue Him. If it was in nature, you may want to go for a walk as you pursue Him. Try to figure out when, where and what elements are key for you in your pursuit of God that lead you into His presence. Then pursue Him in those elements today. Maybe they will become a part of your daily pursuit.

NOTES

WEEK TWO / **DAY SIX & SEVEN**

DAY 6: LET THAT THOUGHT SIMMER

What idea was most challenging this week?

_____

_____

_____

_____

_____

_____

DAY 7: LET THAT THOUGHT SIMMER

What day or concept do you want to rethink about?

_____

_____

_____

_____

_____

_____

WEEK THREE

WEEK THREE / DAY ONE

CHILDLIKE FAITH

[13] "People were bringing little children to Jesus for him to place his hands on them, but the disciples rebuked them. [14] When Jesus saw this, he was indignant. He said to them, 'Let the little children come to me, and do not hinder them, for the kingdom of God belongs to such as these. [15] Truly I tell you, anyone who will not receive the kingdom of God like a little child will never enter it.' [16] And he took the children in his arms, placed his hands on them and blessed them.

[17] As Jesus started on his way, a man ran up to him and fell on his knees before him. 'Good teacher,' he asked, 'what must I do to inherit eternal life?'

[18] 'Why do you call me good?' Jesus answered. 'No one is good—except God alone. [19] You know the commandments: "You shall not murder, you shall not commit adultery, you shall not steal, you shall not give false testimony, you shall not defraud, honor your father and mother."'

[20] 'Teacher,' he declared, 'all these I have kept since I was a boy.'

[21] Jesus looked at him and loved him. 'One thing you lack,' he said. 'Go, sell everything you have and give to the poor, and you will have treasure in heaven. Then come, follow me.'

[22] At this the man's face fell. He went away sad, because he had great wealth."

MARK 10:13-22

I've had a common experience many times over with each of my nine kids. It goes like this. I'm walking past one of my kids who is on something near me. It could be a bunk bed, a set of stairs, a playground, a couch. It's something up off the ground where they are at eye level with me or above me. The next thing I know, without warning, they are flying through the air in my direction. For whatever reason, I always imagine they are thinking they are like spider monkeys soaring through the air to their desired location. In this case, their desired location is wrapping their arms and legs around my head. I've always caught them, but sometimes with quite a shocked look on my face.

Question: Why would they jump without warning? The answer is simple: because Dad is right there and they trust that Dad will catch them. They display a simple level of faith that comes so naturally to them.

There is something about how kids trust and how kids naturally display faith that Jesus highlighted and pointed to while He walked among us.

This week we are focusing on childlike faith and what Jesus meant when He pointed to children as a model for us.

The passage of scripture at the beginning of today's reading often gets separated into two separate stories. We see what seems like two unique encounters. The first is the blessing of the children. The second is the encounter Jesus has with the rich young ruler. While they are two separate encounters, they happen back to back. I think there is something significant for us to learn regarding our faith when we view them as back-to-back moments and compare and contrast how they interacted with Jesus.

Let's start with what's happening in verses 13-16. Children are being brought to Jesus for Him to bless them. Why are people doing that? Well, in Jesus' day it was tradition for fathers to bring their children to the local synagogue, and the elders would join the father in a prayer of blessing. It was a special event in the local community. In these verses, the parents are bringing their children to Jesus, the Rabbi, with the same hope.

The scripture says the disciples are indignant. That means to be angry, annoyed or frustrated. They are feeling this way because they held the cultural view of kids that they should be seen and not heard. Children couldn't produce anything of perceived value for the community, so they were perceived as being unimportant.

Yet Jesus makes a statement over them that seems to fly in the face of the perspective of the day. He says at the end of verse 14, "For the kingdom of God belongs to such as these." We will unpack more of the significance of this statement tomorrow, but for now, what's amazing is how Jesus is pointing to the children as a model for us in faith. He's saying there is something about how they approach God, something in their perspective, something in their demeanor that is critical for us to learn.

Now, compare them with the rich young ruler who will approach Jesus immediately after this moment. He looks like he's got everything together. He's been following the law perfectly since he was a young child. He has wealth, a perceived value to the community, success, probably wisdom and honor among those who know him. Yet, he will leave, walking away from Jesus with his head hung in sadness, because he can't bring himself to follow so innocently, so recklessly, so much like a child.

There is a movie from 2021 called "The Jesus Music." It's a documentary of the journey of contemporary Christian music. I loved it, because it took me back to my childhood and all my favorite Christian bands. But the thing I appreciated most about the movie is the way they told the story of the uphill battle of the Christian rock movement. The foundation of the movement really goes back to Calvary Chapel in Southern California. There was a pastor by the name of Chuck Smith who was boldly proclaiming the gospel. Now there is nothing unusual about that, but what becomes unusual is his willingness to proclaim the gospel to whoever walked in his church without judgment of how they looked. One day a couple of long haired, flip-flop-wearing hippies walked into his church. They heard the gospel, responded, and placed their faith in Jesus. The amazing thing is, first, that the pastor didn't kick them out when they first walked in (which is what most other churches would have done in those days) and second, is that after they gave their lives to Christ, Chuck didn't expect them to cut their hair and adhere to a new dress code to come to church. He actually encouraged them to bring their friends. And that's exactly what happened. Their friends came, long-haired and flip-flopped, and came and came and came. And instead of telling them to cut their hair, put down their guitars and quit their bands, they simply stopped singing about sex, drugs, and rock and roll and started singing about Jesus.

Then Chuck did something incredibly brave that broke all the rules of the day. He put them on the platform and asked them to sing their new songs about Jesus at the youth group meetings. The meetings grew and grew. Thousands were coming. But not thousands of clean-cut kids from mainstream culture. It was thousands of hippies, rebels, and rock-and-rollers. They came because they loved the music, and instead of walking away from their music they simply changed the subject. The new subject was Jesus. And the Jesus music movement was born.

What I love about the history of the Jesus movement in the 70's and 80's is how the musicians embodied childlike faith. They weren't polished or well-put-together. They were raw, honest, come-as-you-are childlike followers of Jesus.

DAILY CHALLENGE: How about you? Have you believed that your faith needed to be polished or perfect before it could be effective? What do you like about the concept of childlike faith? What does it mean to you for your faith to be honest, innocent, raw and real? Who could you live out your faith in front of, or share your faith with today in a very real, honest and authentic way?

NOTES

WEEK THREE / DAY TWO

CHILDLIKE FAITH SIMPLY RECEIVES

[14] "When Jesus saw this, he was indignant. He said to them, 'Let the little children come to me, and do not hinder them, for the kingdom of God belongs to such as these. [15] Truly I tell you, anyone who will not receive the kingdom of God like a little child will never enter it.'"

MARK 10:14-15

My youngest kids still don't fully grasp the value of a dollar. They know that things cost different amounts, but it doesn't make sense why one thing is more expensive than another or how far apart the values of two different items might be. For example, a pack of gum and a box of LEGO bricks cost significantly different amounts. Yet to them, they see it as one pack of gum, or one box of LEGO bricks; can I pick which one I want to buy today? You and I know that's not how it works. But to them, because they can't earn money at their age, all they know is the life of one who simply receives. And they receive whatever it might be (a pack of gum, or a box of LEGO bricks) in the exact same way. They simply receive it.

There is something about that mindset of simply receiving that Jesus is highlighting in this passage in Mark 10. Notice what Jesus says in verse 15, "anyone who will not receive the kingdom of God like a little child will never enter it." Childlike faith begins with this idea of simply receiving.

Let's hop back into the story and context of Mark 10. The families are bringing their children to be blessed by Jesus. Then Jesus drops this bomb of a statement in verse 14, "... for the kingdom of God belongs to such as these." Here's why that is a crazy statement.

To say that the kingdom of God belonged to children ran smack in the face of the Jewish religious system of the day. They were convinced that if you didn't somehow earn your way to heaven by doing good works, then you didn't get to go there. And in their view, children were unable to earn anything because they didn't know the difference between right and wrong yet. If you don't know the difference between right and wrong, how can you do enough right to earn your way into the kingdom of God?

How could Jesus identify someone as a part of the kingdom of God who couldn't do anything to earn it?

With this seemingly insignificant act of blessing these children, Jesus was communicating and emphasizing a radical new idea that can be summed up in one word… grace. Grace is undeserved favor. It is getting what you don't deserve.

The religious leaders in Jesus' day did not see the kingdom of God through the lens of grace. They saw it completely through the lens of the law, a rule-based righteousness in which you could do enough right and earn your way to heaven.

In fact, as you look at the question from the rich young ruler in the following verses, you'll see he carried that same belief. His question to Jesus in verse 17 is, "What must I do to inherit eternal life?" That fourth word in his question is at the heart of his belief system: DO. He believes he has to do something to earn his way into the kingdom of God. Jesus' answer is going to push back against the doing-based faith that those in His culture carried.

Unfortunately, many still see faith through the lens of doing and earning.

Just as Jesus pushed back against this, scripture also clearly pushes back against that idea as well in verses like:

"… not by works of righteousness which we have done, but according to his mercy he saved us… "
TITUS 3:5 (KJV)

"For it is by grace you have been saved, through faith…not by works, so that no one can boast."
EPHESIANS 2:8-9 (NIV)

Let's get practical for a moment. How does this sometimes play out in our faith journey? Well, have you ever wanted to pray for something but you felt unworthy of receiving what you were asking for? It could be a great job, the perfect home for you and your family, or a miraculous healing. You start to think, "Maybe if I serve God better, or love people more, or give more to the church, or read my Bible more faithfully, maybe then somehow I'll deserve my prayer request to be answered."

We do this all the time by creating all these imaginary hurdles that we need to jump over for our prayer to be worthy of being listened to. As if once we DO enough good things, then even if God doesn't answer the prayer request, we were at least worthy (in our minds) of the prayer request being answered.

Childlike faith simply receives. There is nothing you can do to be more worthy of God's grace and goodness in your life. Grace—undeserved favor—is exactly what it is. So when you pray or ask God for something, engage your childlike faith which simply receives, knowing there is nothing you can do to become more deserving or worthy of any additional grace in your life.

Trick-or-treating is a great picture of childlike faith and simply receiving. Every year my kids go trick-or-treating and you know the drill. They walk up to the house and they say, "Trick or treat." Now while they just gave the person two options, they only have one option in their mind. The truth is, no child walks up to the front door of a neighbor's home thinking, "If you don't give me something, I've got a trick that will get you." No, they walk up to the door only expecting the treat. They have done nothing to earn it, nothing to be worthy of it, they simply receive it. We as parents drill only one thing into our kids for that night, and that is to say thank you. Because in the whole process of trick-or-treating, that's the only thing they can bring to the experience. They can bring a heart of gratitude.

In the same way, childlike faith carries this mindset. **There is nothing I can do to earn it, I simply receive it. My heavenly Father likes to give generously and all I can do is express gratitude.**

DAILY CHALLENGE: Do you unintentionally create hurdles in your mind that you need to jump over before you will be worthy of God listening to your prayers? Have you placed conditional restraints upon your faith, that once you do enough, then your faith is deserving? Write down anything you've thought you needed to DO before you could ever ask God for anything. Additionally, make a list of the hopes, dreams and longings for your life. While none of us can do anything to be deserving of these, take them to God today in faith. Present them to Him with the posture of childlike faith that simply receives.

NOTES

WEEK THREE / DAY THREE

CHILDLIKE FAITH SIMPLY BELIEVES

²¹ Jesus looked at him and loved him. 'One thing you lack,' he said. 'Go, sell everything you have and give to the poor, and you will have treasure in heaven. Then come, follow me.'

²² At this the man's face fell. He went away sad, because he had great wealth."

MARK 10:21-22

Have you ever prayed a conditional prayer? It sounds like this: "God if you do (fill in the blank), then I will believe (fill in the blank)." If God provides me with the job, then I'll believe in Him. If God heals my family member, then I'll believe I can trust Him. If God gives me the raise, then I'll believe I can trust Him with my money.

How did that work out for you? It's conditional belief.

That's what the rich young ruler is dealing with in his encounter with Jesus. We could argue that he believes in Jesus. He probably believes Jesus is good. He probably believes Jesus is performing real miracles. He may even believe Jesus is the Messiah (the promised One who would come to be the Savior of the world). But his belief ultimately comes with conditions. He wants to follow Jesus, but he has some things in his life that will get in the way of his faith.

His conditions sound like this: "I'll believe and I'll follow as long as it doesn't throw off the things in my life, impact my values, or push against what I love."

Which is why Jesus' challenge to him pushes against his wealth. Because Jesus knows this is the conditional aspect of this man's faith. He'll believe as long as it doesn't impact that one area of his life. But childlike faith doesn't have conditions of following or conditions of belief.

Childlike faith simply believes. And it believes in big, audacious, illogical and crazy ways.

I love how Mike Yaconelli puts it in his book "Dangerous Wonder." In talking about childlike belief he says this:

> Sneaking into my parents' bathroom, I would find the stash of forbidden towels (the thick, new ones reserved only for guests). Once outside, with the towel tied around my neck and dragging on the dirt behind me, I would run as fast as I could and jump off the highest survivable launching pad I could find. With arms outstretched, cape billowing behind me, wind rushing past my ears, I believed I was flying.
>
> Then came a day when, without warning, without provocation, I woke up, never to wear a "cape" again. Wherever the knowledge came from, it came nonetheless, and from that moment on I knew flying was nothing more than a childhood fantasy. I would never fly … and there is no Superman.
>
> In retrospect, my day of "enlightenment" was a very sad day. I know now that something inside of me died that day. Whatever the "something" was, it was the stuff of dreams and imagination—the place where dancing, singing, laughter, and playing lived. Even at six, I understood that the possibility of flying wasn't the point: it was the aliveness I felt when I thought I could fly…

I love how Yaconelli puts it. While he paints a sad picture, he also captures so well the level of faith that a child has. A child has the ability to just believe, and believe for the impossible.

Jesus' statement about faith like a mustard seed is so profound. "… if you have faith as small as a mustard seed, you can say to this mountain, 'Move from here to there,' and it will move. …"

MATTHEW 17:20

Being able to tell the mountain to move might seem insane, but it is actually an invitation for every believer in Jesus to come back to childlike belief. It's an invitation to put your cape back on and start once again believing for the impossible.

DAILY CHALLENGE: Like the rich young ruler, has your faith or your belief become conditional in any ways? Like the rich young ruler, who didn't want his faith to impact his work or wealth, are there areas in your life that you've kept off-limits from your faith because ultimately you don't want Jesus to challenge you in those areas?

Did you have greater faith when you were a younger child? Have you grown out of your faith in some ways? What steps could you take today to put back on the cape and start once again believing for the impossible?

NOTES

WEEK THREE / DAY FOUR

CHILDLIKE FAITH IS SIMPLY SIMPLE

²¹ Jesus looked at him and loved him. 'One thing you lack,' he said. 'Go, sell everything you have and give to the poor, and you will have treasure in heaven. Then come, follow me.'

²² At this the man's face fell. He went away sad, because he had great wealth."

MARK 10:21-22

A couple of years ago we bit the bullet and bought season passes to a local ski hill. I call it a hill because that's what it is. There are no mountains in the plains of the midwest—we have hills. But at least it's something. And I consider doing anything outside as better than spending your day inside. By having season passes, it meant we needed to outfit our entire family with ski gear. It sounds easier than it is. My wife and I both snowboard, so we had some kids who wanted to try that out, while most wanted to stick with skiing. Of course, there was no way we were going to go out and buy all new gear, which may have been easier, but also way too expensive. So I volunteered to do the work to find all the used gear we needed.

Finding it all was a bigger task than I imagined. Find these boots in these sizes. Find this style of ski at these lengths. Find poles for everyone at every length. Make sure to get a couple snowboards for the kids who want to try them out. We'll need a few pairs of snowboard boots that can fit multiple people depending on who's riding that day. Oh and by the way, everyone should probably have a helmet. So start measuring head circumferences and figure out what size they need and keep in mind they probably have a preference of color. And don't forget goggles for everyone.

Needless to say, I have enough equipment now to outfit just about anyone of any size with either skis or snowboards. And I'll be the first to admit it: it is ridiculous.

It sounded so simple, but it became overwhelmingly complex before I knew it. And this is the pattern of our lives, right? We have a tendency for our lives to become so complex, busy and overwhelming. And I believe the enemy uses this complexity to stunt our faith.

This is where the rich young ruler finds himself. He's grown up and he has become "adultified." In verse 22 it says, "At this the man's face fell. He went away sad, because he had great wealth." The word that gets translated as *great*, is not like *you're great* or *you're awesome*, but it is communicating quantity, vastness, how much or how many. He doesn't have one item of great wealth, he has many items of wealth. His life has become busy, complex, filled with stuff and responsibilities. The things of this world ultimately have his heart… the things of this world have cluttered his heart.

Jesus is asking him to get rid of it all and get back to the basics and follow him.

I will summarize the childlike principle this way: Childlike faith is simply simple.

Sometimes, just like life, we make faith overly complicated when it's not. Jesus' invitation is to drop all the "stuff" and just follow Him. The amazing thing is that if we do the "following" portion of Jesus' invitation, He will sort out all the "stuff" for us.

Yesterday we read a little from Mike Yaconelli in his book "Dangerous Wonder." He continues his thought on childlike belief in saying,

> …it was the aliveness I felt when I thought I could fly; it was the voice I heard deep inside- a warm and loving voice, a living, believing voice, a wild and dangerous voice. Every time I hear that voice, I recognized who it was: God. But that day, when I was just six years young, my God-hearing went bad.

> One sad day, we are aware of an absence. We can no longer hear the God-voice, and we are left with only silence—not a quiet silence but a roaring silence.

We did not want to stop hearing God's voice. Indeed, God kept on speaking. But our lives became louder. The increasing crescendo of our possessions, the ear-piercing noise of busyness, and the soul-smothering volume of our endless activity drowned out the still, small voice of God.

I love that final sentence and how Yaconelli puts it. "The increasing crescendo of our possessions, the ear-piercing noise of busyness, and the soul-smothering volume of our endless activity drowned out the still, small voice of God."

How cluttered has your life become? And has the clutter started to clutter out your faith?

If we were to just silence the noise of life, the complexity of life, and the busyness of life, maybe, just maybe you would discover a God who has been there with you all along. He's been offering things through faith this entire time. He's been offering grace and mercy, peace and love, joy, hope and courage.

I think there are many people who at some point made a decision to follow Jesus years ago, but then life happened. Life got complex. You got hurt. You picked up responsibilities and burdens. You got some scars. You put up some fences around your heart. You became self-reliant. In the process of life, things don't seem as simple as they once were.

Yet, I believe Jesus is calling us back to childlike faith that is simply simple.

DAILY CHALLENGE: Where does your life feel overly complex? Has *"The increasing crescendo of our possessions, the ear-piercing noise of busyness, and the soul-smothering volume of our endless activity drowned out the still, small voice of God"*? How might God be calling you to simplify your possessions, your busyness or your activities?

ADDITIONAL CHALLENGE: Try sitting for five minutes in complete silence. Try not to let your mind wander to your day's activities, responsibilities, or "to do" list. But just be with God. Ask Him to speak into your faith in the quiet simplicity of the moment.

NOTES

WEEK THREE / DAY FIVE

CHILDLIKE FAITH IS ANCHORED IN DAY ONE

"We have come to share in Christ, if indeed we hold our original conviction firmly to the very end."

HEBREWS 3:14

Vince Lombardi is known as one of the most iconic individuals in the NFL. He's considered by many to be the greatest coach in football history. But one of the things that he famously became known for was something that he did on the first day of the season every year. He would take his team, sit them down, hold up a football and say, "This is a football."

It seems silly that an NFL football coach would make such an obvious statement to a group of grown men who had been playing the sport for years and were now professionals. These are guys who have eaten, breathed, slept and lived football more than anyone else on the planet and he is holding it up in front of them, and telling them about the ball as if they've never seen one before. Why?

It's because he wanted to bring things all the way back to the beginning. He wanted to take them back to the basics and the fundamentals of the sport.

Sometimes when we think about our faith, we think about growth, moving forward and taking next steps. And while all of that is important, there is something so profound that will move your faith forward: and that is going back. Specifically going back to the beginning of your faith.

In Hebrews 3:12-13 it says, *"See to it, brothers and sisters, that none of you has a sinful, unbelieving heart that turns away from the living God. But encourage one another daily, as long as it is called 'Today,' so that none of you may be hardened by sin's deceitfulness."*

I think all of us would agree that we do not want to end up with unbelieving hearts that turn away from God. No one sets out on their faith journey with that as their intention. Yet that's where many end up. So the author of Hebrews is giving some insight as to how to avoid that fate.

He tells them to encourage one another daily so their hearts and minds won't be hardened by the lies that sin tells. Which by the way, if you think you can make it through this life on fire for Christ while only directing your attention toward God once a week (on Sundays), you're likely on a trajectory toward failure. Hebrews says you and I are going to need encouragement daily, not once a week, not periodically, not when things seem most discouraging, but daily. Just like we eat daily to give our bodies the nutrition we need to live a healthy life, we need to feed our spiritual lives with daily encouragement to keep us from falling for the many lies that our sinful surroundings are shouting at us.

Hebrews continues in the next verse to say, "¹⁴ We have come to share in Christ, if indeed we hold our original conviction firmly to the very end."

What does that mean? It means if we want to make it to the end of our lives well and share in all that Christ has for His children, we need to hold to our original conviction to the very end.

What was your original conviction? What he's referring to is your faith on day one.

I love how the New Living Translation puts it:

"For if we are faithful to the end, trusting God just as firmly as when we first believed, we will share in all that belongs to Christ."
HEBREWS 3:14 (NLT)

He's saying there is something so profound about your faith on that day when you first believed. Hebrews challenges us to trust God as firmly as you did on that first day. And if you do it well, it will actually carry your faith all the way through to your very last day on planet earth.

What was unique about your faith on day one? Your faith that day was so simplistic, so childlike, so all-in. It was filled with complete surrender, because you didn't know how to do it any other way. **There is nothing more childlike than the day you give your life to Christ.** On that day, you're just a "baby Christian." Your faith is in infancy, but at the same time, it is completely full and perhaps in its richest state.

Have you ever known someone (this could be your story) who made a decision to follow God at camp, at church, at a concert or a conference? They had what felt like a mountaintop moment between them and God. Then they came home and their faith seemed to drift away. As it drifted they may have even said, "I think I had just made an emotional decision at that time, and now it's over."

I would argue that while, yes, it felt emotional, those were genuine emotions as a result of genuine faith. It is incredibly emotional for anyone surrendering everything to Jesus. But it wasn't just hype or manipulation, it was childlike faith. And there is nothing more energizing than childlike faith. This is why the author of Hebrews tells us to go back and hold onto that form of faith. If you do, you'll find childlike faith that is so rich, it will continue to energize your faith all the way to the end of your life.

DAILY CHALLENGE: If you're not a Christian, think about the first moments in your life when you tested faith to any degree. What was it like? If you're a Christian, think back to the day that you trusted Jesus as your Lord and Savior. Do you remember what your faith felt like that day? If you don't remember, ask God to give you an impression on your heart of what your faith was experiencing at that time. Write down some of the attributes of your early faith. Now ask God to re-energize your faith today with the level and wonder of childlike faith you carried long ago.

NOTES

WEEK THREE / DAY SIX & SEVEN

DAY 6: LET THAT THOUGHT SIMMER

What idea was most challenging this week?

DAY 7: LET THAT THOUGHT SIMMER

What day or concept do you want to rethink about?

WEEK FOUR

WEEK FOUR / DAY ONE

BELIEF AND UNBELIEF

[17] "A man in the crowd answered, 'Teacher, I brought you my son, who is possessed by a spirit that has robbed him of speech. [18] Whenever it seizes him, it throws him to the ground. He foams at the mouth, gnashes his teeth and becomes rigid. I asked your disciples to drive out the spirit, but they could not.'

[19] 'You unbelieving generation,' Jesus replied, 'how long shall I stay with you? How long shall I put up with you? Bring the boy to me.'

[20] So they brought him. When the spirit saw Jesus, it immediately threw the boy into a convulsion. He fell to the ground and rolled around, foaming at the mouth.

[21] Jesus asked the boy's father, 'How long has he been like this?'

'From childhood,' he answered. [22] 'It has often thrown him into fire or water to kill him. But if you can do anything, take pity on us and help us.'

[23] ' "If you can"?' said Jesus. 'Everything is possible for one who believes.'

[24] Immediately the boy's father exclaimed, 'I do believe; help me overcome my unbelief!'

[25] When Jesus saw that a crowd was running to the scene, he rebuked the impure spirit. 'You deaf and mute spirit,' he said, 'I command you, come out of him and never enter him again.'

[26] The spirit shrieked, convulsed him violently and came out. The boy looked so much like a corpse that many said, 'He's dead.' [27] But Jesus took him by the hand and lifted him to his feet, and he stood up."

MARK 9:17-27

Tamara Baker tells this unbelievable story. "When I was around eight, my dog followed my dad to wait with me for my school bus. While they were waiting, my dad saw Fluffy get hit by a truck, so he took him and buried him. We then went out of town for the weekend. But on Sunday evening when we got home, Fluffy was standing on our porch! Dad couldn't believe it and told us, 'I buried him on Friday!' Turns out, Fluffy had just been knocked out cold, so he dug himself out of the grave and waited for us to come home."

Sometimes we use that word "unbelievable" to describe what seems so unlikely, so difficult to believe. But the root of that word, which is "unbelief," and the idea of unbelief may be the thing that is hindering your faith.

In Mark 9, we see an encounter with a man, his son, Jesus, and a crowd. In verse 19, Jesus calls out something unique. He says, "you unbelieving generation." He doesn't say, "you of little faith" or "why do you not believe?" Instead he calls them "unbelieving."

Then in verse 23 he drops a huge statement, "Everything is possible for one who believes."

So here we have this contrast between unbelief and belief. Jesus says they are an unbelieving generation and then says everything is possible with belief.

Now the father's response is probably the best and most insightful part of this story, and his response is probably a perfect representation of what you and I might be feeling in many situations.

"Immediately the boy's father exclaimed, 'I do believe; help me overcome my unbelief!'"
MARK 9:24

Meaning, I do have belief (faith), but I also have this thing called unbelief. I have both. The problem is, I need help to overcome the thing that is sabotaging my belief (faith). And the thing that is sabotaging my faith, making it ineffective, is called unbelief.

Let's define things further. What's the difference between a lack of faith and unbelief? Sometimes they get meshed together, but they are very different. A lack of faith means it's not there. There is simply an absence of faith. Unbelief is actually something that is working in opposition to your faith. The "un" prefix means to come against.

A simple example would be if you tie a knot and then you untie it. If you untie it, then you are undoing it. You are reversing that which you did. So if I have belief, but then also unbelief, I am undoing what I did.

Unbelief is the purposeful undoing of faith.

Picture it like this. Imagine there is a pool. And in the pool there is a small toy sailboat floating in the middle. The sailboat represents any situation that you're praying about in life. It is the thing that you want your faith to have an impact upon. When we pray in faith about our situation it is like pointing a fan at the sailboat and it begins to blow that sailboat across the pool. We are actually seeing our faith have a real impact upon the situation. But then, on the opposite side of the pool there is another fan (or even two or three fans) blowing against the sailboat. They are blowing the sailboat back toward the middle of the pool and sabotaging the effectiveness of the first fan. Those fans that are blowing against the sailboat are unbelief. They are any lie or concept that comes against the truth of who God is or who He says we are in Christ Jesus.

A simple example of what those fans could be, that are sabotaging our faith, could be lies like the following:
"God has more important people to listen to than me."
"I sinned last week and even though I asked for forgiveness, I still feel guilty and I know God's not listening to me."
"I'm praying about this situation, but I really don't think anything will happen."

These are the types of thoughts and ideas that feed unbelief.

This is a big deal because Jesus makes it a big deal. He makes it the whole issue. He says this is the heart of your problem: "You unbelieving generation." And then He says, "Everything is possible for one who believes."

This week we're going to focus on unbelief and how it can sabotage our faith. Perhaps it's not that you lack faith, perhaps you have a problem with unbelief that is negating the effectiveness of your faith. It is **undoing** what your faith is **doing** in your life.

DAILY CHALLENGE: How can you relate to the statement of the father who said, "I do believe, but help me overcome my unbelief?" Let's see if we can discover roots of unbelief in us. If unbelief is any lie or concept that is coming against the truth of who God is or who He says we are, what lie or concept is fostering unbelief in your life?

NOTES

WEEK FOUR / DAY TWO

UNBELIEF:
WHAT ELSE IS GROWING IN YOUR GARDEN?

3 "'Listen! A farmer went out to sow his seed. 4 As he was scattering the seed, some fell along the path, and the birds came and ate it up. 5 Some fell on rocky places, where it did not have much soil. It sprang up quickly, because the soil was shallow. 6 But when the sun came up, the plants were scorched, and they withered because they had no root. 7 Other seed fell among thorns, which grew up and choked the plants, so that they did not bear grain. 8 Still other seed fell on good soil. It came up, grew and produced a crop, some multiplying thirty, some sixty, some a hundred times.'"

MARK 4:3-8

When Lisa and I were newly married, the first real home we lived in was a small little farm house on 10 acres of land. While we didn't own the home or the land, our landlord gave us a lot of freedom to use the land as we wanted. So we decided to plant a small garden. Both Lisa and I grew up in homes where our parents and grandparents always had gardens, so the idea of growing our own vegetables seemed logical and simple enough.

We chose a piece of property that was simply grass and weeds and rototilled the land until it looked ready for planting. We picked our seeds and planted our garden. A week went by and little green shoots started sprouting up all over the garden. We were excited to see what this would produce. We continued walking out to assess the progress of our garden every day. However, we quickly realized we had a problem. We were looking at all this greenery coming out of the dirt, but we couldn't discern the rows that we thought we had planted. There were sprouts coming up in every square inch of our garden. What we didn't know was when we rototilled the ground, we simply mixed up the dirt with whatever was already in the soil. We didn't know better, but we had simply planted our seeds surrounded by grass, weeds, and whatever else was in the soil.

Needless to say, we didn't get any fruit or vegetables from our garden that year. The garden became this massive mixture of plants and weeds and it ultimately produced nothing at all.

Jesus tells the parable of the seeds in Mark 4. In it the seed represents the Word of God, the gospel, and the soil represents different states of people's hearts.

I heard Pastor Bill Johnson connect this parable to the idea of unbelief and I think it is worth considering the principles of the parable in how they relate.

Jesus goes on in a later verse to explain the parable and what the different conditions of the soils represent. I want to zero in on one of Jesus' explanations.

[18] "'Still others, like seed sown among thorns, hear the word; [19] but the worries of this life, the deceitfulness of wealth and the desires for other things come in and choke the word, making it unfruitful.'"

MARK 4:18-19

I want to make the argument that in the same way that there are things from this world that choke out the ability for these seeds to produce fruit, that is how unbelief chokes out belief.

We have this thing called unbelief. It can be the distractions of the world or lies of this world. But what happens is it chokes out the fruitfulness of our faith. It's not that our faith is not present. In the parable, the seed actually grows, it just doesn't produce fruit. In the same way, I think there are many Christians whose faith is actually present, but the problem is the weeds of this world (which foster unbelief) choke their faith, so no fruit can be produced.

Another way of saying it is: **There are many Christians who have genuine faith, but they also have a whole lot of genuine thorns** that they are purposefully watering, that are growing up beside their faith, choking it out from being effective.

And we wonder why our faith is ineffective.

It's because we are watering GARBAGE in our garden.

If you listen to trashy music, and watch trashy things on TV, and listen to trashy advice from friends, and allow the trash and the lies of this world to permeate your life and you actually water those things, it shouldn't surprise you when you find unbelief choking out the effectiveness of your faith.

We shouldn't wonder why our faith is ineffective when we water the thorns beside our faith. We shouldn't be shocked if our faith seems under attack when we willingly water the weeds that sabotage our faith.

DAILY CHALLENGE: Ask yourself what else is growing in your garden? Do you water your faith on Sunday but then water the weeds in your life Monday through Saturday? What are the potential weeds in the garden of your life? How do you plan to weed your garden?

NOTES

WEEK FOUR / DAY THREE

UNBELIEF:
LIES ABOUT YOURSELF

"Then I heard a loud voice in heaven say:

'Now have come the salvation and the power

and the kingdom of our God,

and the authority of his Messiah.

For the accuser of our brothers and sisters,

who accuses them before our God day and night,

has been hurled down.'"

REVELATION 12:10

I want to continue what we talked about yesterday about assessing what is growing in your garden. For the next few days we'll take a deeper dive into some of the common ways the enemy is trying to plant those thorns beside your seed of faith. When we learn to identify the thorns, it becomes easier and more obvious where they are and how they need to be dealt with.

Today we're going to be talking about the thorns which are lies about yourself. Tomorrow we'll be talking about the thorns that are lies about God. What's the difference?

Lies about yourself are lies that attack your character and your abilities. Lies about God are lies that attack His character and His abilities.

For today let's dive into the lies about yourself.

In Revelation 12 we see the final demise of Satan. That is going to be one SWEEET day!

But we are not there yet. While the enemy has ultimately lost the war at the cross and Christ's resurrection, he is still picking fights, trying his best to steal, kill and destroy all that he can before his final demise.

I picture it a bit like a king who has been in battle and he and his army have clearly been defeated, but not yet captured or brought to justice for their war crimes. As they are running for their lives they are burning every town and village along the way, trying to destroy as much as possible in their retreat. If they can't rule it, they don't want the new king to have anything good in the land they have lost. That's what the devil is doing. He's burning everything he can and doing his best to make everyone's lives miserable as he's running from Jesus who defeated him.

In his efforts to make everyone's lives miserable he has one primary tactic that he uses to try to destroy us. He tells lies. In fact in Revelation 12 it describes what Satan has been doing all this time. It says, "For the accuser of our brothers and sisters, who accuses them before our God day and night." That is what he's doing. He's accusing you day and night. He's lying to you day and night.

What do these accusations sound like? They are the thoughts that come to the forefront of your mind that usually starts with a "you" statement. They sound like this:
"You will never be good enough."
"You will never be forgiven for what you did."
"You'll never have what it takes to serve God effectively."
"You'll never have victory over your addiction."
"You don't know enough of the Bible, you don't pray enough, you're not spiritual enough."
"You'll never have a good friend. You'll never be a good friend."
"You're ugly."
"You're fat."
"You're worthless."
"You are… you are…you are…"
You get the idea.

These accusations are against who God created you to be and who He says you are.

While Satan might have been the one who planted those thorns (lies) in our gardens, our problem is that not only do we NOT pull the thorns, we sometimes water them. We start repeating these lies that Satan spoke over us. And every time we do so, we actually water the lie. It springs up beside our faith and starts to choke out our faith and limit its fruitfulness.

The band Lost And Found wrote a song years ago called "Rachel Racinda" that captures so well how a lie can hold one captive. It's a sobering and sad song. Check it out.

> Rachel Racinda's small sister Melindas
> had come to the end of her rope
> trying and vying and sighing and crying
> and dying to meet the boy Hope
>
> but Melindas stayed firmly and tightly secure
> inside her house where her life could be sure
> the windows were bolted and doors they were locked
> and every day Hope came to visit and knocked
> but Rachel Racinda's small sister Melindas
> made certain the entrance was blocked
>
> he couldn't come in and she couldn't come out
> no matter how loudly she'd scream and he'd shout
> the walls were too thick and the glass was too strong
> and even though both of them knew it was wrong
> Rachel Racinda's small sister Melindas
> had been in her house for too long
>
> she saw herself ugly and called herself dumb
> but Hope had seen beauty and brilliance and fun
> the world was too scary she wouldn't partake
> but Hope talked of what a fine leader she'd make
> she lowered the shade and she fastened the curtain
> her future was scary and love was uncertain
> Rachel Racinda's small sister Melindas
> knew all she had known was at stake

no matter how Hope begged her please to come out
she valued her fears and she trusted her doubt
and soon even she couldn't open the lock
or break out the window or turn back the clock
or let Hope come inside and show her his care
her house was too solid, her house was despair
And Rachel Racinda's small sister Melindas
was used to her life and stayed there

she talked of adventure, but dreamed from inside
and most of the days, well she slept or she cried
and even though Hope and the others had tried
Rachel Racinda's small sister Melindas
learned early and well how to hide

When the lies (or thorns) become so deeply rooted in one's life, it's hard to see anything different. But what we must do is remind ourselves it's just a lie. It may be a lie that we've watered for a long time, but it is still just a lie. It is just an accusation. And the thing that overcomes and weeds out the lies is truth. As I'm sure you've heard John 8:32 quoted before, "'Then you will know the truth, and the truth will set you free.'"

Speaking truth over yourself is the most effective gardening tool that you have that will come against the accusations of the enemy. So let's get to our gardens and start pulling the thorns of accusations out today.

Why? Because as we deal with these thorns, we are actually weeding out the things that cause unbelief, which sabotage our faith.

DAILY CHALLENGE: What do the accusations of the enemy sound like in your life? Write the words "thorns to be pulled" in your notes. Below it, write a few accusing "you..." statements that you feel are often in your garden. Below the accusation statements, write a few truth statements of who God made you to be, or who He says you are that come against those lies.

NOTES

WEEK FOUR / DAY FOUR

UNBELIEF:
LIES ABOUT GOD

"Now the serpent was more crafty than any of the wild animals the LORD God had made. He said to the woman, 'Did God really say, "You must not eat from any tree in the garden"?'"

GENESIS 3:1

Yesterday we started diving into our gardens to start identifying the thorns (or lies) that the enemy has planted. We looked at lies about ourselves. Today we'll look at lies about God. I described the difference between the two this way:

Lies about yourself are lies that attack your character and your abilities.

Lies about God are lies that attack His character and His abilities.

These often can sound very similar but they are separate in who they are attacking. For example, "You're way too much of a sinner" is a lie that attacks you. While "God would never forgive that sin of yours" is a lie that attacks His character and His promises.

Both lies can foster unbelief and undermine your faith. And the enemy will be generous in planting as many lies as he's able, hoping for you to water any of them.

We see this tactic of telling lies about God as the very first strategy of the devil. It is his way to come against the relationship between God and mankind. It's found in Genesis 3.

Satan comes in the form of a snake and approaches Eve. His very first words ever spoken to mankind come in the form of a question that undermines the word of God. He asks, "Did God really say…?" In other words, "you should question God and what He says." And then Satan misquotes God. "Did God really say, 'You must not eat from any tree in the garden'?"

Eve will go on to correct Satan and say, "We may eat fruit from the trees in the garden, but God did say, 'You must not eat fruit from the tree that is in the middle of the garden'…" (Genesis 3:2-3)

Then Satan will go **from questions to contradicting.** In verse 4, Satan replies, "You will not certainly die."

Here, he ups his game. Instead of just questioning God, Satan contradicts God by saying what God says is not true. But it doesn't stop there. He takes it one more step. In verse 5 he plants a lie about God. "'For God knows that when you eat from it your eyes will be opened, and you will be like God, knowing good and evil.'"

So he actually plants a lie about the motives of God and character of God. As if God is desperately trying to hide something from Adam and Eve and keep it all to Himself.

So he goes from questioning, to contradicting, to accusing.
And he does the same thing today. It might sound like this:
Questioning: Did God really say you shouldn't live with your boyfriend or girlfriend?
Contradicting: He didn't say that… you can't find that anywhere in the Bible. (Side note: in scripture, moving in with one another happens only in the context of marriage between a man and woman, see Genesis 2:24.)
Accusing: The standards of God are just old-fashioned, they are probably no longer relevant to me.

Or here's another:
Questioning: Did God really say you shouldn't party?
Contradicting: He didn't say that, in fact, doesn't the Bible say somewhere "eat, drink, and be merry, for tomorrow we die." (Side note: yes it says that in Ecclesiastes 8:15, but that would be misapplied, misquoted and completely out of context.)
Accusing: God enjoys His existence to the fullest, why does He not want that for me? Why is He trying to keep me from letting loose sometimes to enjoy life to the fullest?

The point is, Satan is using the same tactics he's always used to try to surround your faith with thorns (lies) about God that will choke out your faith.

Yesterday all the lie statements were against you. Here's how the lie statements often sound when coming against God.

God can't be trusted.
God may love the world, but He doesn't like you very much.
God can forgive everything, with the exception of that one thing you did.
God can't use you after you sin.
God only speaks clearly to pastors and missionaries; no wonder you struggle to hear the voice of God.
God only uses super spiritual people, and you're not one of them.
God only works in the lives of the lucky ones, and you're not one of them.
God only protects other people.
God only blesses other people.
God only brings peace to other people.
And so on.

These are just some of the accusations that come against the character of God and the promises He's made to us.

One of the ways I experienced this growing up was in my view of what God was capable of. I grew up not believing in all the gifts of the Holy Spirit. Specifically, those gifts that are referred to as the sign gifts. Things like speaking in tongues, prophecy, and healings.

I've come to a place where I believe these gifts are still able to be practiced and useful within the church. Let me just use miraculous healings as an example. What's bizarre is that in my church setting growing up, we actually believed God had the power to heal miraculously, it was just rare and more like a fluke that happened now and then. My belief today is that miraculous healings are readily available and we expect to see them often.

Here's how that lie about God's abilities acted like thorns that choked out my faith. I remember being in prayer meetings when I was younger and someone would say, "Pray for my family member who has cancer, that they would be healed." We would pray for their family member, but I don't think a single person in the room believed God would do it. I know I didn't. If I pray for something not believing that God could or would do it, then what I actually have is unbelief that is sabotaging my faith.

Now that this thorn has been removed from my belief system, it no longer chokes out my faith in that area. As a result, I see many more healings on a more frequent basis.

DAILY CHALLENGE: What do the lies about God often sound like in your life? Once again write the words "thorns to be pulled" in your notes. Below it, write a few lies about God that you feel are often in your garden. Below those statements, write a few truth statements about who God is and His promises to you, to come against those lies.

NOTES

WEEK FOUR / DAY FIVE

UNBELIEF: UNATTENDED DOUBT

[24] "Now Thomas (also known as Didymus), one of the Twelve, was not with the disciples when Jesus came. [25] So the other disciples told him, 'We have seen the Lord!'

But he said to them, 'Unless I see the nail marks in his hands and put my finger where the nails were, and put my hand into his side, I will not believe.'

[26] A week later his disciples were in the house again, and Thomas was with them. Though the doors were locked, Jesus came and stood among them and said, 'Peace be with you!' [27] Then he said to Thomas, 'Put your finger here; see my hands. Reach out your hand and put it into my side. Stop doubting and believe.'"

JOHN 20:24-27

Have you ever doubted God? If you're like most everyone I know, including myself, then your answer is probably yes. Doubting God or questioning God is a natural part of the spiritual journey.

The question is not whether you doubt God or question God at some point in your life. The question is, what will you do in that season as you doubt? Will you allow that season of doubts and questions to drive you toward truth and toward God, or will it result in the watering of thorns in your garden which will choke out your faith?

In John, we get a front row seat to a disciple who is going through his own doubting process. Unfortunately this moment becomes a labeling moment for him. He will forever be referred to as "doubting Thomas." Poor Thomas. While doubting is a part of his journey, he will go from doubting to deep conviction. My prayer for you and me is the same: If and when we go through seasons of doubt, may God lead us through to the other side, that we may emerge with true and deep Biblical convictions.

Notice what happens with Thomas. He says outright in verse 25, "Unless I see the nail marks in his hands and put my finger where the nails were, and put my hand into his side, I will not believe."

Sometimes we picture Thomas like he's just a doubter, but notice what he's in pursuit of. He is in pursuit of Jesus and seeing Him fully. It's like he wants to press in deeper than just taking someone's word for it. He wants to chase after Jesus in such a way that will remove all doubt.

Unfortunately, I don't think most people approach their doubts like Thomas. I don't think most are desiring to press further into scripture and know Jesus more intimately. Instead, I think most will phone a friend or search on the internet if they have a doubt or question. The problem with that is if you allow the internet, or your friend's opinion, or culture to help form your belief about God when in the midst of doubting, you will likely find yourself watering thorns as opposed to watering seeds of faith.

There is a movement right now in culture that I would caution you about if you find yourself exploring it. It is the deconstruction of faith. There are many books that have been written about the subject and it may be the fastest growing movement in western culture in regard to faith.

The idea of deconstruction is simply this: it is taking apart that which formed our faith, specifically in areas that may have been off track or theologically incorrect. Deconstruction has become a term that has become synonymous with embracing those who question and those who doubt.

Now before you think I simply oppose everything that has to do with deconstruction, I do not.

However, I will say the vast majority of people that I have known who are "deconstructing" are truly not deconstructing at all. They are actually demolishing. Demolition and deconstruction are two very different things.

Deconstruction is the dismantling of something. In this case, what one wants to dismantle is anything that was not true in their past faith journey. Demolition is the destruction of something. And in this case many (while they call it deconstruction) are actually simply throwing out their faith completely and rebuilding their faith however it seems fit to them. That is not a healthy way to deconstruct anything.

What's funny is there is nothing new under the sun. Lisa and I each went through phases of the deconstruction of our faith back in the day. We just never called it that. We called it unlearning. But it was the same thing. We had to unlearn some things that were theologically incorrect and rebuild them with truth through the process of diving deep into the Bible, seeking God as well as godly advisors, and shoring up our faith in truth.

Years ago I had a guy come to me in my church and say, "I'm leaving the church." I was shocked as he had been a regular attender, he had served in many different capacities, and while we had many tough conversations surrounding questions he had in the Bible, he was an all around solid guy. I asked Him, "What's going on?"
To which he replied, "I did something this week."
"What did you do?" I asked.
"I decided to assume everything I've always believed was a lie. I embraced that idea all week long. And now I just don't think I believe in God anymore."

It's not that he just doubted, or asked a few hard questions. Instead he purposed to water and nurture the thorns of unbelief. Should we be shocked that he lost his faith? We really shouldn't be. He embraced the process of watering thorns which in turn choked out his faith.

DAILY CHALLENGE: How do doubts and questions about God hit you? How have you dealt with them in the past? Do you look for answers from your friends or Google or from scripture and a greater pursuit of God? What subject do you need to study in the Bible to answer your doubts or your questions and water the seeds of your faith?

NOTES

WEEK FOUR / DAY SIX & SEVEN

DAY 6: LET THAT THOUGHT SIMMER

What idea was most challenging this week?

DAY 7: LET THAT THOUGHT SIMMER

What day or concept do you want to rethink about?

WEEK FIVE

WEEK FIVE / DAY ONE

PERSISTENCE WHEN THINGS DON'T SEEM FAIR

[1] "Then Jesus told his disciples a parable to show them that they should always pray and not give up. [2] He said: 'In a certain town there was a judge who neither feared God nor cared what people thought. [3] And there was a widow in that town who kept coming to him with the plea, "Grant me justice against my adversary."

[4] 'For some time he refused. But finally he said to himself, "Even though I don't fear God or care what people think, [5] yet because this widow keeps bothering me, I will see that she gets justice, so that she won't eventually come and attack me!"'

[6] And the Lord said, 'Listen to what the unjust judge says. [7] And will not God bring about justice for his chosen ones, who cry out to him day and night? Will he keep putting them off? [8] I tell you, he will see that they get justice, and quickly. However, when the Son of Man comes, will he find faith on the earth?'"

LUKE 18:1-8

My kids have a phenomenal ability to continue to push on a subject until they get their way. It can sound like asking for ice cream, wanting to have pizza and a movie, a desire to go out on the boat in the summertime, or hit the hills skiing in the winter. Whatever it is, when they have something on their minds that they deeply desire, they have a tendency to ask, and ask, and ask, and ask. They demonstrate a level of persistence that I think all of us actually need in our faith. While their persistence may seem a bit obnoxious, that's actually an accurate reflection of what Jesus seems to point to when telling parables about persistent faith.

This week we're going to be focusing our attention on the idea of persistence in our faith. These two things, persistence and faith, are clearly connected. We see this in multiple places in scripture. Right here in Luke 18, verse one Jesus is telling this parable to show His disciples "that they should always pray and not give up." That's persistence. Then in verse eight,

He concludes the thought by asking a question: "… when the Son of Man comes, will he find faith on the earth?" That's faith.

Meaning, the persistence modeled in the parable is a reflection of the persistence that should accompany our faith.

So let's consider the parable and the model. In the parable, there is a judge who doesn't seem like a very good judge. He is simply described as not fearing God or caring what people think. If one didn't fear God it was assumed they lacked a moral compass. If they didn't care what people thought, it was assumed they lacked compassion and empathy. So here we have a judge who lacks a moral compass and lacks compassion and empathy. With that attitude, how can they make good judgment calls?

There is a widow who simply keeps coming and begging for justice against her adversary. We don't get any more details in the story about her adversary or how she was being mistreated. We just know she is facing injustice, because that is what the judge decides to do for her in verse five. He says, "yet because this widow keeps bothering me, I will see that she gets justice."

Injustice is any place where you feel like "life is not fair."

Where does life not seem fair to you?

It could be the job you didn't get, the bill you didn't deserve, the loved one you lost too early, the promotion that passed you by, the child who made life at home impossible, the spouse who didn't hold up their end of the promises, or the accident or illness that has caused so much pain in your body. It's these situations in life where you feel like "life is not fair."

Last week I walked out to my driveway and noticed my car that my kids drive had been hit. The front bumper had a dozen cracks and portions missing. It was clearly a small fender bender where either one of my teen drivers ran into something, or someone ran into my car. I asked my kids who drive the car if they hit something that caused the damage. They all said no. My problem is because I don't look at the car every day, I have no idea when the damage really took place. I have no idea where the damage took place. I have no idea how it happened. So here I have a thousand dollars' worth of damage and no one to blame and no one to pay for it. This is the nature of injustice in the world. It's where life just doesn't seem fair. I did nothing to deserve this, yet it has come to me all the same.

So what do we do in those moments? **Jesus actually challenges us to engage our faith in those moments.** And not just engage our faith, but actually to "up our faith" in those moments. It's a challenge to pray more persistently. It's a challenge to trust more audaciously. **It's a challenge to pursue God constantly with a heart that longs to see justice.**

For me, even with the damage to my car, here's how my prayer sounds. "God, restore to me that which was taken. Somehow, bring justice to what feels like an unjust situation. Provide either finances or a way for the car to be fixed, that is not at my expense."

Now the real question is will I keep praying that prayer? Or will it be a one and done prayer? God is looking for the persistent ones. He is responding to the ones who demonstrate persistent faith.

That final question of "will He find faith on the earth?" is a good question for us. Can God find the kind of faith He describes in this parable in us?

I don't know where life has felt unfair to you. But I believe verse seven applies to us in the same way. "And will not God bring about justice for his chosen ones, who cry out to him day and night?... I tell you, he will see that they get justice..."

Don't be afraid to cry out persistently to Him to bring you justice. It's a prayer worth praying and faith worth growing.

DAILY CHALLENGE: Where have you experienced injustice in your life? God's justice may not look exactly like you'd expect, but the ones who exercise persistent faith will experience His justice. Maybe there have been a couple things that you've never prayed for or stopped praying about in your life. Are there one or two things that you want to purposely bring back to God and see Him bring justice to? Engage your faith and start praying about those today.

WEEK FIVE / DAY TWO

PERSISTENCE TO MEET YOUR NEEDS

[5] "Then Jesus said to them, 'Suppose you have a friend, and you go to him at midnight and say, "Friend, lend me three loaves of bread; [6] a friend of mine on a journey has come to me, and I have no food to offer him." [7] And suppose the one inside answers, "Don't bother me. The door is already locked, and my children and I are in bed. I can't get up and give you anything." [8] I tell you, even though he will not get up and give you the bread because of friendship, yet because of your shameless audacity he will surely get up and give you as much as you need. [9] So I say to you: Ask and it will be given to you; seek and you will find; knock and the door will be opened to you.'"

LUKE 11:5-9

My boys have a tendency to tear through their clothes pretty quickly. They are just boys. They play hard and nonstop. The worst is when we buy them a new pair of jeans and on the second day they come walking into the house with a hole in the knee. I ask, "What happened to your new jeans?" And they respond, "Oh, I didn't even notice… I don't know." So it shouldn't surprise me when they run out of clothing so quickly.

I remember feeling pretty bad when one of my boys came to me and asked, "Dad, can I have a second pair of shoes?" I was thinking, don't we have bins filled with shoes, and tons of hand-me-downs to rummage through? But I was wrong. Yeah, we had bins full of shoes (mostly girls shoes), but when it came to the boys, they just tore through their clothing and left nothing for the next in line. So sure enough, he only had one pair of shoes, and they were falling apart. I felt horrible that here my son was begging for just one pair of shoes that weren't falling apart.

Lisa and I just didn't realize it and as soon as we did we took him out to get a new pair. Why? Because meeting our child's basic needs is something we naturally want to do. And our hearts hurt for him and with him as he came to us begging for another pair.

In the same way, God's heart is to meet your needs as well.

In Luke 11, Jesus tells another parable. It has some similarities to the parable we looked at yesterday and some differences. In today's parable, we've got an individual who has a friend who shows up after a long journey. It's late at night, but the individual wants to be a good host and feed their guest, but he has nothing to give. So he goes to his neighbor at midnight and knocks on the door for help.

Now, if you had a neighbor show up at your front door at midnight asking for some milk and a loaf of bread, you probably would think they are crazy too. You might shoo them away like the neighbor in the parable. But it goes on to say, the individual has "shameless audacity" in their request. And because of their shameless audacity the neighbor gets up and provides as much as the individual needs to host their friend.

What seems crazy to me is that in both yesterday's parable and today's the individuals seem overly obnoxious. They seem annoying and bothersome. Yet, this is the trait that Jesus is elevating here. **This persistence in conjunction with faith is the key to seeing your faith make a difference.**

I don't know if you've ever thought to yourself, "I don't want to come across to God as if I'm overly needy or annoying." As a result, you don't bring your request to God with persistence. I know I've done this many times. I make my request to God sounding like this, "God, this what I need or want; you have a perfect plan, and so I trust you with it." Now, it sounds very respectful and humble. But those are not the traits God highlights here. He doesn't say, "because of the man's respectful and humble request the neighbor got up and met his needs." It says because of the man's shameless audacity, he got up and met his needs.

Now, I never want to pretend as if I can be bossy to God, and I'm sure you don't as well. However, I also don't want to undersell my desires and my needs to God in an effort to come across as respectful and humble. God knows the state of your heart, and it is right to approach the throne of God with great respect and humility. But once there, there is no point in sugarcoating your needs, go ahead and ask with shameless audacity. Knock on the door of heaven with shameless audacity today knowing that God is a good heavenly Father who is happy to meet your needs.

DAILY CHALLENGE: Write down 2-3 needs in your life. How have you prayed about those things in the past? Jesus actually points to shameless audacity as a model of how to best engage our faith. Today, ask, seek, and knock on the doors of heaven. See how God responds to shameless audacity.

NOTES

WEEK FIVE / DAY THREE

PERSISTENCE IN DESPERATION

"Then he stretched himself out on the boy three times and cried out to the
LORD, 'LORD my God, let this boy's life return to him!'
[22] The LORD heard Elijah's cry, and the boy's life returned to him, and he
lived."

1 KINGS 17:21-22

Have you ever been desperate in life? You probably have at one point or
another. It could sound like any of these statements:
I'm desperate for a raise or I won't be able to afford my rent.
I'm desperate to pass my exam so I can pass my class.
We're desperate to get pregnant, we've been trying for so long.
I'm desperate to get an answer to my medical issue.
I'm desperate to find a way out of my addiction.
I'm desperate to find a healthy relationship.
I'm desperate to land the contract or my business will go belly up.
What is your "I'm desperate for…" statement?

Today we shift to another person in scripture who models persistent
prayers. The guy we're looking at is Elijah. Elijah was an Old Testament
prophet whose job was to speak on behalf of God to the people and the
king in his day. The king in Elijah's day was Ahab. And Ahab was a
pretty wicked and godless king. Elijah's message to Ahab was (and I'm
paraphrasing) "because of Ahab's wickedness and the wickedness in the
land, there will be a drought in the land until Elijah says differently." After
delivering that message, Elijah went into hiding. He found himself staying
with a widow and her son. God was miraculously providing for them so
they were able to stay alive and stay fed. Near the end of Elijah's time with
the widow, her son became sick and died.

The whole nation was in a place of desperation with the drought. But now
there was a different level of loss and desperation that came upon this
widow. In that day and age, women's rights were not the same as they are

today. Without a husband, a woman couldn't fully provide for herself or her needs. This woman's son was not only her precious loved child, he was also her future provision. Once grown, he would provide for her for the rest of her life. Without him, she faced a destitute, hopeless future.

She and her son had become a safe haven for Elijah during those years of hiding out. Now desperation came upon them. And Elijah did the strangest thing. He laid the child down, and "then stretched himself out on the boy three times and cried out to the Lord". I don't fully understand the "why" behind all this. Why he stretched himself over the boy versus just laying his hand on the boy's shoulder. Why three times versus just once. Why the boy died in the first place versus being healed when he was sick? I don't know the "why", I just know the model.

Elijah modeled something for us in his desperation. He modeled persistence with his faith on this occasion.

While he might have been alone in that room praying for the boy, I can't imagine how silly he might have felt stretching out over the boy as he cried out to God. Then to do it a second time, and a third… I wonder if Elijah felt foolish in his request. Regardless, he kept going for it. He kept praying and kept crying out.

When things are desperate, how do you pray?
Do you pray with persistence in your desperation?
There are times when I have wept in prayer and times I laid flat on my face before the Lord. There have been times I've fasted and prayed in desperation and times when I sang in worship as a form of desperate prayer. Whatever the case may be, I never looked back and regretted going "all in" in my desperate prayers. God has always produced something in me in those moments as something shifts and grows in my faith.

Things don't always end up the way we want. But it doesn't change the model. There is something that grows in our faith during times like these. There is growth when we pray with great persistence in seasons of desperation.

If you've grown weary of praying in your season of desperation, might

I encourage you to stretch yourself out a few more times. God is doing something. It may be through you, it may be in you, but just like in Elijah's life, God is doing something.

DAILY CHALLENGE: What is your desperation statement? Your "I'm desperate for..." statement? How have you been praying about that situation? Let's try to stretch our faith today as we "stretch out" in desperation.

NOTES

PERSISTENCE IN THE BIG PICTURE

⁴¹ "And Elijah said to Ahab, 'Go, eat and drink, for there is the sound of a heavy rain.' ⁴² So Ahab went off to eat and drink, but Elijah climbed to the top of Carmel, bent down to the ground and put his face between his knees.

⁴³ 'Go and look toward the sea,' he told his servant. And he went up and looked.

'There is nothing there,' he said.

Seven times Elijah said, 'Go back.'

⁴⁴ The seventh time the servant reported, 'A cloud as small as a man's hand is rising from the sea.'

So Elijah said, 'Go and tell Ahab, "Hitch up your chariot and go down before the rain stops you."'

⁴⁵ Meanwhile, the sky grew black with clouds, the wind rose, a heavy rain started falling and Ahab rode off to Jezreel."

1 KINGS 18:41-45

In the fall, there's always a day when it's time to do our last-minute yard work before the first snow. This is when we try to get all our leaves raked and out to the road. You might ask, "Why wait until the last minute"? Here in Wisconsin, it seems like that's the only way it ever works. The last of the leaves don't seem to fall off the trees until the day before the first snowfall. Basically, on that day of yard work it's usually cold and miserable.

It usually goes the same way every year. I rally the whole family together and convince them that if we work hard we can get all the work done quickly and be back inside soon to warm up. So we head out, with rakes, a leaf blower, and tarps to haul loads of leaves where they need to go. And without fail the same thing happens every year. Before we know it, a few kids are raking piles of leaves together in random purposeless locations. Instead of raking the piles onto the tarps and hauling them to the road, the kids are jumping into the piles, burying each other in the piles, and throwing leaves at each other. The younger kids have ventured off to something a little more creative. They are raking leaves into lines on the ground and pretending they are outlines to homes and rooms within their homes. As I approach them they say, "Dad, walk in the doorway over there into our house. Look at the kitchen I made and my bedroom is over here." They are even starting to bring their blankets and pillows outside to put in their leaf-outlined bedroom. Two other kids have the leaf blower and have ceased to blow leaves and instead are blowing each other in the face. They are laughing hysterically at how their faces look with the air filling their cheeks and their hair blowing in the wind like rock stars. I look around and think, has everyone forgotten what we are doing here? Did everyone forget what the big picture was?

Sometimes in our prayer life we have a tendency to pray about the things that seem most relevant to us (it's our little leaf pile we are focused on). We pray about the place where we feel injustice, we pray about our needs, we pray about our places of desperation. But what about the big picture? I think many of us lose sight of persistent prayer in regard to things that pertain to the big picture. It's the bigger things that God is up to in our neighborhood, in our community, in our state, in our nation, and in our world.

Today we return to the account of Elijah. We're skipping a lot, but in short, Elijah comes back, confronts Ahab, has a showdown with Ahab's false prophets, and wins. After the victory, the final thing Elijah needs to do is to turn the water back on that has been off for so many years. There has been a complete and total drought in the land for years, and now Elijah is going to ask God to restore the rains. This is the bigger picture of God demonstrating His power to the whole nation through Elijah.

So Elijah goes to the top of Mount Carmel and starts praying for rain. As he's praying he asks his servant to go and look for rain clouds in the distance. Time after time, Elijah's servant comes back and says, "there are no rain clouds on the horizon." Elijah continues to pray and continues to say, "go look again." Seven times Elijah tells his servant to go out and look for rain clouds.

I don't know about you, but at what point would you start wondering about your prayer? On the third time, fourth, fifth, sixth? I can imagine there is some major faith stretching happening here. He's already told Ahab to go get ready, because the rain is coming. But there is a big picture win happening here. There is a bigger move of God that Elijah knows God is up to. He knows that he needs to continue to pray until it comes to fruition.

There are places in our world where I believe it's important for us to consistently contend in prayer until it comes to fruition. These are places where we are praying for the bigger Kingdom win. We are praying with God's big picture in mind.

Let me give you some examples:
When we drive by a local business and pray God's blessing over them, that's a big picture community prayer request.
When we pray for our local teachers and superintendents in our school districts, that's a big picture community prayer request.
When we pray for our local first responders, that's a big picture community prayer request.
When we pray for government leaders and policies that they are proposing, that's a big picture community, state level, or even national prayer request.
When there is drought in a state and we start praying for God to release the rain over our land to bless our farmers, that's a big picture state-wide prayer request.
When we pray for fires happening out west or floods happening down south, those are big picture national prayer requests.
When we pray for revival in the land, that's a big picture national and global prayer request.
When we pray for the war to cease that's happening in Ukraine, that is a big picture global prayer request.
The point is there are big picture prayers that I believe we should be persistently praying.

Sometimes, we get so focused on our little leaf pile that we forget that God has a big picture plan that is at work. And we have the opportunity, like Elijah, to persistently pray for the bigger Kingdom work that is at hand.

DAILY CHALLENGE: Write down one big picture Kingdom win for your community, then your state, your nation, and then the world. Start praying about those big Kingdom wins daily. Make it a part of your daily prayer time to persistently pray about things you know that are on God's heart and in line with His bigger Kingdom work.

NOTES

WEEK FIVE / DAY FIVE

PERSISTENCE... LITTLE BY LITTLE

²² "They came to Bethsaida, and some people brought a blind man and begged Jesus to touch him. ²³ He took the blind man by the hand and led him outside the village. When he had spit on the man's eyes and put his hands on him, Jesus asked, 'Do you see anything?'
²⁴ He looked up and said, 'I see people; they look like trees walking around.'
²⁵ Once more Jesus put his hands on the man's eyes. Then his eyes were opened, his sight was restored, and he saw everything clearly."

MARK 8:22-25

The band Queen sang a song called "I Want It All." The final line of the chorus is simply, "I want it all, and I want it now." Unfortunately, that's the only way most of us want our prayers to be answered. We want the entire thing answered and we want it answered now. We struggle to even imagine another option, or an incremental option.

I remember a time years ago, when Lisa and I were in desperate need of paying our mortgage for the month. We prayed faith-filled prayers asking God to provide for us to be able to pay the mortgage. Later that week we found an envelope with cash in our mailbox. But it wasn't for the amount of our mortgage. It was only about a third of what we needed. Do you think I was mad for it not being the amount we needed? No, Lisa and I were actually blown away and so thankful for the miraculous provision. However, we were still short. So we kept praying. And God provided. I don't remember exactly how that need got met, but I do remember it was miraculously covered. It just wasn't all at one time, all in one moment.

This is part of the process in learning to grow our faith. It is learning persistence in our prayers, and being grateful in the little-by-little provisions.

What's bizarre is even Jesus modeled this. In Mark 8:22-25, a blind man is brought to Jesus. His friends are begging Jesus to heal him. So Jesus spits in the man's eyes (that's really weird, right?) and then asks, "Do you see anything?" The man replies by saying (my paraphrase) that he partially sees. So Jesus touches his eyes a second time and then his sight is fully restored.

It's strange to me that this even happened with Jesus. If there was ever someone who could just heal completely and heal right now, it was Jesus. So why does it take persistence with Jesus' faith for the healing to take place?

Here are two possible reasons.

First, it could be a model for us. Just like the financial provision for our mortgage, when God brought that to us incrementally and continued to grow our faith along the way. There have also been times when I've experienced incremental healing just like in Mark 8. This has happened when I pray for people with migraine headaches. After I pray, I ask, "Do you feel any better?" People will often respond with, "Yes, although I still have a little headache, it definitely got better." In which case, I'll always pray for it one more time. Sometimes the headache goes away a little more, and sometimes completely.

Second, it could be to play a part in our faith journey. Notice in Mark 8 it says that the friends of the blind man brought him to Jesus and begged Jesus to heal him. It was not the blind man himself who was begging to be healed, but his friends who were begging. Is it possible that the two-part healing is to grow the faith of two different groups of people? The first group is the friends who express their faith in Jesus and desperation on behalf of their friend. The second is the blind man himself. Perhaps after he's able to partially see, this second half of the healing is really about engaging and growing his faith.

In fact in those headache situations I imagine the same is often true. Maybe the initial relief of their headache is more a reflection of my faith, but the second relief of pain or the complete healing of their headache is more a reflection of their faith as it engages in the process.

I don't know what it is you need today, but I encourage you to be grateful for the little-by-little. God often works in incremental ways. I know you want it all, and you want it now. But God may just have a little now and a little later. This is the way our faith often grows as we pray persistently and embrace the little-by-little.

DAILY CHALLENGE: Where do you need God to show up in your life? Ask God to show up even in a small way. When you see God's hand at work, thank Him for what He's done. Don't get frustrated for what He hasn't yet completed. And then, press on and persistently ask for more.

NOTES

WEEK FIVE / DAY SIX & SEVEN

What idea was most challenging this week?

What day or concept do you want to rethink about?

WEEK SIX

MOVED HEARTS: FOR THE WEAK AND POWERLESS

¹² "On the day the LORD gave the Amorites over to Israel, Joshua said to the LORD in the presence of Israel:

'Sun, stand still over Gibeon,

and you, moon, over the Valley of Aijalon.'

¹³ So the sun stood still,

and the moon stopped,

till the nation avenged itself on its enemies,

as it is written in the Book of Jashar.

The sun stopped in the middle of the sky and delayed going down about a full day. ¹⁴ There has never been a day like it before or since, a day when the LORD listened to a human being. Surely the LORD was fighting for Israel!"

JOSHUA 10:12-14

Have you ever started crying because someone else was crying? It happens pretty regularly for me. I'm not afraid to admit that I'm a pretty sensitive guy and I'll cry in an emotional part of a movie, or tear up when others shed some tears. If it ever happens on a Sunday, I usually get scolded by at least 10 people after service who will say, "You did it to me again–every time you start to cry, I start to cry." That's never my goal, it just happens. But it is also just the way humanity is hard-wired.

Since we are made in the image of God, it would make sense that our ability to sympathize with others is actually a God-ordained attribute. As such, it would also make sense that the way our own hearts are stirred in faith would make a real impact upon the Lord.

I've often said it this way: "Moved hearts move the heart of God."

If we want to see our faith become more impactful, a question we might want to ask is, "Is my heart moved?

2 Samuel 21:14 says, "They buried the bones of Saul and Jonathan his son in the country of Benjamin in Zela, in the grave of Kish his father; thus they did all that the king commanded, and after that God was moved by prayer for the land." (NASB)

Many Bible translations translate that final line in the verse as "God answered prayer on behalf of the land." However, the Hebrew word that gets translated as "answered prayer" is *athar* which more accurately is translated "moved by prayer."

So God can actually be moved or impacted by our prayers and by our faith. The question this week is, where do we see acts of faith that move the heart of God?

Are there situations where God's heart is naturally moved?

Are there things we can learn from those encounters that we can apply to our faith?

Today we consider a situation where I believe God's heart is naturally moved: the area of defending the weak and the powerless.

In Joshua 10, Joshua has led the people of Israel into the promised land and they have already conquered the first two of many cities. This causes fear throughout the land where the Amorites are located (a group of people, cities, and kings within the promised land). The Amorites wanted to conquer the city of Gibeon which was a large and important city in the land. Five Amorite kings came together to conquer Gibeon. Gibeon had made a peace treaty with Joshua and the Israelites, so they called out to Joshua for help. Joshua arrived on the scene with his entire army to defend the Gibeonites from the attack of the Amorites.

In the middle of that attack the armies were so large and so vast, there was no way to defeat them all in one day, so Joshua prayed a bizarre and faith-filled prayer. He prayed that the sun and moon would stand still until Gibeon was avenged. And that's what happened. In verse 13 it says, "The sun stopped in the middle of the sky and delayed going down about a full day."

Can you imagine that? It probably felt like being in Alaska (or any far-northern country) in the summertime. The sun never seems to set, it just spins around in the sky. But in this case the sun just stopped. It stopped because God was responding to a request from Joshua that was centered around fighting for the underdog. It was about defending the weak and the oppressed. Joshua's heart was stirred for the underdog, so he prayed the impossible prayer. And God listened. Why? Because God's heart is moved by the hearts of those who pray faith-filled prayers to defend the weak and powerless.

Psalms 82:3 says, "Defend the weak and the fatherless; uphold the cause of the poor and the oppressed."

There are situations in life in which I believe we are "set up" for major faith-filled prayers to be answered. One of those situations is praying in faith for the weak, the oppressed, and the powerless.

As I write this, the war in Ukraine is entering the second month. This has been a war where Russia is attacking the weak and powerless. If you consider how Ukraine is outgunned and outmanned, they should never have lasted this long. I've been praying for Ukraine every day. I continue to pray what may be considered to be ridiculous prayers, however, I believe they are in line with the heart of God. They are prayers that fight for the weak and the oppressed. Some of those prayers sound like this: "God, stop the Russian soldiers from following orders that would take the lives of the innocent. Keep bombs from detonation, protect the people, and thwart the plans of the oppressors."

I read an article earlier this week titled "U.S. assesses up to 60% failure rate for Russian missiles." In the article it goes on to talk about how over half of the Russian missiles are landing without detonating. At the same time, I've watched videos coming out of Ukraine of church pastors where they are walking into the town square and a bomb is sticking half out of the ground having not detonated. The pastor says something to the effect of, "This is happening everywhere in Ukraine, it is just God's grace to us, He is protecting us."

Is it possible that faith-filled prayers from around the globe are defending the weak and the oppressed?

If there is ever a place you'd like to grow your faith and pray huge faith-filled prayers, praying for the weak and the powerless is a great place to start. May our hearts be moved for them, and in turn move the heart of God on their behalf.

DAILY CHALLENGE: Is there an oppressed people group that your heart has always longed to help? What mountain of opposition stands before them? How could you pray for that mountain to be moved on their behalf? What "sun stand still" prayer could you pray today to fight for the weak and the powerless? Is there something the Lord is calling you to do, to get involved and defend the oppressed?

NOTES

[11] "As long as Moses held up his hands, the Israelites were winning, but whenever he lowered his hands, the Amalekites were winning. [12] When Moses' hands grew tired, they took a stone and put it under him and he sat on it. Aaron and Hur held his hands up—one on one side, one on the other—so that his hands remained steady till sunset. [13] So Joshua overcame the Amalekite army with the sword."

EXODUS 17:11-13

I'm grateful to have the days of youth group "all-nighters" behind me. Those were the events where our goal was to keep the kids up all night long. The nights were filled with games, team challenges, strobe lights, food, and a good movie. Hindsight is 20/20 and now looking back, that was really a cruel joke being played on everyone involved. We as youth leaders were completely shot the next day. The kids were being sent home completely sleep-deprived and useless to their parents on their day off. And parents were being required to wake up early themselves and pick up their children at 7 a.m. on their one day off. Talk about a situation that everyone is regretting.

But I remember my family and the kindness they always showed me the day after an "all-nighter." I would come home at 8 a.m. and hop into bed. Lisa would work hard to keep the kids quiet for me all morning as I was sleeping. I would roll out of bed in the early afternoon and they would make a nice lunch for me. Even though I had gotten a few hours of sleep my whole body just felt "off." For the whole day I was always useless and felt like I was walking in a fog. The kids would come and rub my back and help me with my chores, and really just carry me through the day.

Have you ever needed that in life? Have you ever needed someone to come alongside you and help carry you through the day, the week, or the season you were in?

Do you know someone like that, or have someone in your life who could really use someone to come alongside them? If you do, you have the perfect opportunity to grow your faith and exercise faith-filled prayers that naturally move the heart of God.

In Exodus 17 Joshua is leading the Israelites into a battle against the Amalekites. Moses, the leader of the Israelites, heads to the top of the hill overseeing the battlefield. He takes the staff of the Lord with him (verse 9). This is the staff the Lord used to convince Pharoah to let the Israelites go. This is the staff the Lord used to part the waters of the Red Sea. This is the staff that has represented the power of God going with His people. So now, Moses is going to hold that staff above his head throughout the battle. As long as the staff remained in the air, the Israelites were winning, but when Moses' arms grew tired and that staff lowered, the opposing army started winning the battle. So "Aaron and Hur held his hands up—one on one side, one on the other—so that his hands remained steady till sunset. So Joshua overcame the Amalekite army with the sword."

This is such a beautiful picture of the power of partnering. There are times when we don't have what it takes to win a victory alone. It doesn't mean you're not set up for a victory, it just means it was always designed to be a group victory. I believe this is the case we see here with Aaron and Hur.

What's interesting is Aaron and Hur also display faith in this moment. This is not simply Moses' faith at work, but Aaron is believing in the God of the Israelites and Hur is as well. They are putting their faith into action by holding up Moses' arms. Together as a group of three, they are able to last until the end of the day. A feat that probably none of them could have handled alone was able to be tackled as a group… as partners.

Ecclesiastes 4:12 says, "Though one may be overpowered, two can defend themselves. A cord of three strands is not quickly broken."

There is power in numbers and power in partnership. Just like Ecclesiastes says, "A cord of three strands is not easily broken," when you learn to partner your faith with others, you'll discover God will use it to grow your faith and use it for greater impact. He will use it to make an impact that could not have been made alone.

I've been in many prayer settings where I believe breakthrough happened because we were praying as a team. We were partnering together. One of those occasions happened in my house when we lived in Minnesota. We had been experiencing what I could only describe as severe spiritual attacks over our family. So we invited a prayer team over to partner with us and pray for us. One individual would pray something distinct and purposeful in one room that truly only applied in that exact space. We would walk to another room and immediately another team member would pick it up and take the prayer in another direction praying about things that had taken place in that room that no one from the team knew about. And it was passed from one person to the next, and from one room to the next until we had prayed through the entire home. We did this until we as a group felt like we had accomplished what we needed to accomplish.

Afterward, all the spiritual attacks stopped. Our family experienced peace that we hadn't experienced in years. The crazy thing is, I was one of the pastors at the church. I had years of ministry experience. I had been praying for my family throughout the entire time that we had been experiencing spiritual attack. Yet we had not experienced a breakthrough. What changed? The difference is we experienced how faith can move the heart of God when partnering with one another.

As individuals prayed about things in my home which I had overlooked, my faith grew. As others prayed very specific prayers for individuals in my family, my faith grew. As the Lord revealed things to the prayer team, the team's faith grew. The point is, if you want to move the heart of God and grow your faith, try it in partnership with others.

If you're in a small group, pray together out loud. If you have a close friend who is a Christ-follower, share your prayer request with each other and pray for each other together.

This is why at the end of our services we always invite people to come and pray with one of our prayer partners. There is something that grows faith when we partner with others in prayer.

I can't tell you how many times my faith has been encouraged simply by hearing other people pray. Some pray with great passion, others pray with great authority, some pray about things you might be afraid to say, and others pray with a voice of grace and mercy. Each of those flavors of prayers when prayed together and partnered together, collectively and exponentially move the heart of God.

DAILY CHALLENGE: Do you have an Aaron or Hur in your life? If not, the most important thing you do today might be to take a step toward getting into a small group or into community with other Christians. Reach out to someone today to find out about getting into a Christian group so you regularly have people to partner with. For a practical experiment today, think of one other Christian you can practice this with today. Call them, share with them the "mountain that needs to move" in your life, and partner together with them in prayer. Afterwards, write down some of your thoughts or reflections from trying this.

NOTES

....

....

....

....

....

MOVED HEARTS:
PUSH AGAINST ALL LIMITS

22 "A Canaanite woman from that vicinity came to him, crying out, 'Lord, Son of David, have mercy on me! My daughter is demon-possessed and suffering terribly.'

23 Jesus did not answer a word. So his disciples came to him and urged him, 'Send her away, for she keeps crying out after us.'

24 He answered, 'I was sent only to the lost sheep of Israel.'

25 The woman came and knelt before him. 'Lord, help me!' she said.

26 He replied, 'It is not right to take the children's bread and toss it to the dogs.'

27 'Yes it is, Lord,' she said. 'Even the dogs eat the crumbs that fall from their master's table.'

28 Then Jesus said to her, 'Woman, you have great faith! Your request is granted.' And her daughter was healed at that moment."

MATTHEW 15:22-28

The weather in Lake Geneva, Wisconsin, during the early summer of 2021 was very unusual. It was nearing the end of June and all the grass in my yard was starting to turn brown and die. Our area is typically green and lush during that time. I know a handful of farmers and I knew they were in crisis mode. I also have a couple of kids who work at local farms, so I found myself more concerned about the planting season and the lack of rainfall than I would have been in the past. One morning I found myself looking at the 10-day forecast with 10 days of sun and not an ounce of rain on the horizon. I was thinking to myself, this is not good for our farmers, for our community, and least important (but still made it into my thoughts), my grass.

As I was sitting there thinking about this mini-drought we were in and the unfortunate situation this was placing all our local farmers in, the Lord brought a story to mind. It's actually a story we looked at last week. The story of Elijah praying for rain to be released over the land after years of drought. A thought came to my mind. If Elijah prayed for rain to come in a time when the forecast was not 10 days, but hundreds of days of no rain, why couldn't I?

So that's what I did. I prayed and prayed and prayed some more. Just like Elijah who prayed seven times until the first rain cloud formed on the horizon, I just kept going for it. I prayed for what felt like the equivalent of praying seven times for something. Eventually, I felt like I was done. So I finished and went about my day. Later that afternoon, I got home from work and looked out my back door. In the distance there were dark clouds that appeared to be moving our way. I thought to myself, those look dark enough to be rain clouds, I wonder if we might actually get a little bit of rain. So I pulled out my weather app. The same app that I looked at early that morning where we had 10 days of sunshine now showed 10 days of rain. Every day had rain in the forecast. I turned to my wife and held up my phone to her. I told her about my prayer time that morning. Now, I can't claim that I am the only reason why rain came to our area. I'm sure there were hundreds of farmers and folks with personal gardens praying for rain. But for me, my faith grew that day. My faith grew as I prayed for things that pushed against the limits of all logic and common sense.

In today's reading we see another individual who models that same type of faith, and her faith is rewarded. In fact, there are only a few places in scripture where Jesus calls out certain individuals and highlights their faith as being special. This is one of those moments. Jesus points this out when He says to her, "Woman, you have great faith! Your request is granted."

Let's see how her faith is pushing against all the limits.

The very first verse about her reveals the most central aspect of this story. In verse 22, it says she is a Canaanite. The most simplistic implication of that was she was not Jewish. Not only was she not Jewish, the Jews had a pretty strong disdain for the Canaanites. In fact, non-Jews were considered so unspiritual that even being in their presence could make a person ceremonially unclean. Jesus' coming was first and foremost a fulfillment to promises that had been made to Abraham, Issac, Jacob, and David. He is the fulfillment of the promise to bring deliverance to the nation of Israel. So Jesus' ministry was first and foremost for the Jewish nation. He would eventually extend his ministry beyond the Jews, but at this time, it seemed to be outside the limits of His calling.

He has what appears to be a very offensive conversation with this woman where it seems like He refers to her as a dog. However, before you assume the worst, let's see what Jesus was doing here.

It was actually common for Jews to refer to Gentiles (non-Jews) as dogs. When doing so they would use a specific Greek word. That word was Kuon. Kuon meant "wild cur." It was a derogatory term. However, when Jesus refers to taking the scraps and throwing them to the dogs, he uses a different word. He uses the word Kunarion, meaning "small dog" or "pet dog." This was actually a more endearing term. So Jesus is not referring to the woman as an unspiritual person or unclean animal, but a term that carried kindness with it, while still communicating His priority mission from God to the children of Israel.

Jesus is also testing her intentions. Is she just looking for a handout, or does she actually have faith in Jesus? Is this truly faith in action? She passes the test with her response. She acknowledges Jesus' primary mission and acknowledges that she is outside of that mission. But, with grace and persistence, she still asks for the rules to be broken and for the grace and the power of God to be extended to her daughter in spite of her nationality.

Jesus sees her faith for what it is. It was genuine and it was pushing against the limits in ways that even the disciples weren't imagining. Because of her moved heart, Jesus' heart is moved and He responds by healing her daughter.

I think there is something that moves the heart of God in a unique way when we ask for that which we know defies all logic and common sense. When we ask for things that push against all the natural limits, we are speaking a Kingdom language that so rarely is on display this side of heaven.

I've said it this way before. **We need to pray prayers that make God sweat.**

Now, I know there is absolutely nothing you or I could ask that is actually beyond His abilities or remotely difficult for Him to pull off. Nothing we could ask will actually make God sweat. But the idea is this: do we ask for things that seem logical and so normal that perhaps they don't require any faith at all? Or do we ask for things that push all the limits and require great faith? Do we ask for things that seem impossible, that stretch our faith and push the limits?

DAILY CHALLENGE: What seems completely illogical to pray for? If your faith could push against any limits in this world, what would you ask for? Sometimes we pray very doable prayers. What's the prayer request that would "make God sweat?" Those are the prayers that move the heart of God and grow our faith.

NOTES

MOVED HEARTS:
ANCHORED IN AUTHORITY

⁵ "When Jesus had entered Capernaum, a centurion came to him, asking for help. ⁶ 'Lord,' he said, 'my servant lies at home paralyzed, suffering terribly.'

⁷ Jesus said to him, 'Shall I come and heal him?'

⁸ The centurion replied, 'Lord, I do not deserve to have you come under my roof. But just say the word, and my servant will be healed. ⁹ For I myself am a man under authority, with soldiers under me. I tell this one, "Go," and he goes; and that one, "Come," and he comes. I say to my servant, "Do this," and he does it.'

¹⁰ When Jesus heard this, he was amazed and said to those following him, 'Truly I tell you, I have not found anyone in Israel with such great faith.'

¹³ Then Jesus said to the centurion, 'Go! Let it be done just as you believed it would.' And his servant was healed at that moment."

MATTHEW 8:5-10, 13

A few days ago, one of my kids got pulled over by a police officer for rolling through a stop sign. Luckily, only a warning was issued. I've taught my kids to treat police officers with the highest respect. I know not every police officer is perfect, but the vast majority are putting their lives on the line to protect us and uphold the law. With this in mind, they deserve our thanks, our respect and our honor. And when it comes to being pulled over, I've told my driving kids to be respectful, be helpful, be honest, and honor their authority.

When one honors authority, there is often a natural response: the desire to work with the individual who extends the honor.

It works that way when being pulled over, and it works that way for me as well. When people show me honor and respect my authority at our church, I always desire to work with them as well.

This is the principle we are looking at today that moves the heart of God. God's heart is moved when anchored in authority.

In Matthew 8 a centurion approaches Jesus with a request to heal his servant. He models something in this encounter that causes Jesus to point out this man's faith. He makes this statement about the centurion: "Truly I tell you, I have not found anyone in Israel with such great faith." That's a pretty strong statement. Jesus has been traveling with His disciples, with other followers, with the Pharisees and the teachers of the law, and of all the people, Jesus says this guy has the greatest faith of anyone. That's amazing. So what does he have that displays such great faith?

Let's look at the encounter. First off, he's a centurion. A centurion was a commander of 100 Roman soldiers. He would have carried great respect, honor, and authority wherever he went. People would have treated him well and he would have been well off in life. Hence, that's why he had servants.

I love that Jesus offers to go to the centurion's house to heal the servant. What's astounding is how the centurion's faith is on display from the very get-go. He replies to Jesus, "I do not deserve to have you come… But just say the word, and my servant will be healed."

He goes on to give Jesus a lesson in authority (which is funny). But what he is really doing is communicating with Jesus how he perceives authority to work. He basically says, "people obey and respect my authority as a centurion as I lead my troops; I'm sure it's the same way with you. Sickness must obey your authority and do what you tell it to do because you have the power to do it."

He sees Jesus, His power, and His authority in such simplistic and black-and-white terms. His faith is anchored in what he knows Jesus can do. And as such, his faith moves the heart of Christ and Jesus heals the servant that very moment.

The centurion has such confidence in what Jesus can and will do. His faith is so impressive to Jesus that Jesus can't help but respond to it.

There is a scene in the movie "The Lord Of The Rings" where Gandalf is riding into town with his horse and carriage. The kids all come running out to see the fireworks that always follow Gandalf. He seems to just pass by without anything happening. The kids are disappointed and seem shocked that nothing happened. Then at the last minute, fireworks shoot out from his carriage, Gandalf smirks, and the kids burst out with joy and laughter.

In many ways the kids only have one view of Gandalf, and that is that he produces fun and laughter. Because they have such a solid belief he will produce it, he can't help but give them what they know he has and what he is capable of.

I know it's a far stretch to compare Jesus to Gandalf. But in many ways the centurion is like the children following behind, believing with all they are that this wizard will do what he is capable of doing. And Jesus is like Gandalf, who just can't help but respond by showing off who He is and what He is capable of.

Jesus has all authority. And the heart of God is moved when His authority is honored. In fact, if you want to see your faith grow, anchor your heart to his authority and ask with great expectation around things that God has authority over. You'll find he often just can't help but be moved by hearts that are anchored to His authority.

Are you anchored to His authority? This is when you have a black-and-white belief in Him and His abilities.

Let's get practical. What could this look like? To step into this type of faith, I'll sometimes pray prayers that sound "bossy." Before you condemn me, what I'm trying my best to do is have faith anchored in authority. For example, I might pray, "God, you will bless my children and my children's children, according to your promises and your unfailing love." This is just scripture that I'm quoting back to God. Or "God, you will provide my every need in ways that will blow my mind and inspire others to follow you." Once again this is declaring the promises of God's word over my life with authority.

Once again, I'm not trying to come across as bossy. Instead, I'm using language that stretches my faith and declares a belief in Him and His abilities that without that level of declaration just doesn't communicate it for me.

DAILY CHALLENGE: Where in your life do you need God to show up? Find some verses in scripture that speak toward this need. Now pray those verses as a declaration over your life and your situation. Pray those verses anchoring your faith to His authority and His abilities.

NOTES

MOVED HEARTS:
RIDING THE WAVE OF FAITH

[18] "Some men came carrying a paralyzed man on a mat and tried to take him into the house to lay him before Jesus. [19] When they could not find a way to do this because of the crowd, they went up on the roof and lowered him on his mat through the tiles into the middle of the crowd, right in front of Jesus.

[20] When Jesus saw their faith, he said, 'Friend, your sins are forgiven.'

[21] The Pharisees and the teachers of the law began thinking to themselves, 'Who is this fellow who speaks blasphemy? Who can forgive sins but God alone?'

[22] Jesus knew what they were thinking and asked, 'Why are you thinking these things in your hearts? [23] Which is easier: to say, "Your sins are forgiven," or to say, "Get up and walk"? [24] But I want you to know that the Son of Man has authority on earth to forgive sins.' So he said to the paralyzed man, 'I tell you, get up, take your mat and go home.'

[25] Immediately he stood up in front of them, took what he had been lying on and went home praising God."

LUKE 5:18-25

When I was in college, my roommate was a surfer from Delaware. He and I still chat periodically and he still surfs regularly. When it came time for his college graduation, he asked for a pretty unique graduation present. He asked for a paid trip for himself and some of his friends to go surfing in Costa Rica. And that's what we did. Four of us loaded up a bunch of his surfboards and flew to Costa Rica for a week of surfing. Now, I had never been surfing before, but how hard could it really be? REALLY HARD: that's the answer you're looking for. I'm a pretty natural athlete, but I struggled with surfing. I spent most of that week being thrown around by the waves, getting caught in crazy tides, and even at one time catching a wave that brought me crashing down way up on the beach. As I lay there in the sand, I thought to myself, "these waves are crazy." I'm pretty sure you are supposed to catch the wave, but often I think the wave caught me and just threw me where it wanted to.

That's the nature of a wave: whether you catch it or it catches you, if you're in it, you're going with it. Faith can work the same way. You can catch faith, and sometimes faith will just catch you.

But the circumstances that surround those moments are worth becoming aware of and trying to maximize.

In Luke 5, we see Jesus' heart is moved once again by some individuals. They bring their paralyzed friend to Jesus for healing. But there is no way for them to get to Jesus as the house where Jesus is teaching is too crowded.

So they do the unthinkable. They start ripping through the roof of the home to lower their friend at the feet of Jesus. Before you start thinking, that must have made more sense in Jesus' day... you're wrong. Ripping apart people's homes was frowned upon in the same way it would be today. There is no setting in which their actions make sense. This is extreme and unruly. We know this based on Jesus' response. Verse 20 says, "When Jesus saw their faith, he said, 'Friend, your sins are forgiven.'" Meaning this was as extreme in their day as it would be today. What Jesus sees in the friends is their faith.

The Pharisees see Jesus' forgiveness of sin as blasphemy, but that's His point. He is establishing Himself as the Son of God and as equal with God.

In the end, He will heal the man plainly by telling him to pick up his mat and walk.

One of the most amazing aspects of the story is whose faith is talked about. Notice it is not the paralyzed man's faith that is highlighted. It is the friends' faith. It's amazing that the group of friends and their faith stirs the heart of Jesus and brings about the healing.

In many ways, the paralyzed man got picked up by the wave of faith and rode it to his healing. He didn't catch the wave, the wave caught him. And the wave was created by his friends.

But check this out: we know how the man left. He walked home praising God. Meaning he might have gotten picked up by the wave of faith, but he left with his own faith now stronger. He left riding his own wave.

I've experienced both aspects of this story in my faith journey. I've experienced riding the wave of other people's faith and I've experienced creating the wave and watching others be impacted by my faith. In any case it all starts because someone's heart is extremely moved on behalf of another. They are reaching out to God and begging God on behalf of another. They are figuratively willing to rip through anything to get their friend to Jesus. That level of faith moves the heart of God. That level of faith is creating waves. That level of faith produces growth.

So let's get practical. Sometimes the easiest way to put things like this into practice is to imagine the scene for yourself. If I'm praying for someone, sometimes as I pray for them I imagine the process of literally ripping through a roof. That's not a one-minute prayer. I pray for them as long as it would take me to literally get through a roof. With each sentence I pray, I imagine pulling up shingles, tar paper, nails, chopping through wood. I eventually imagine peering through a small hole, then a larger hole, and finally a hole large enough to lower my friend down through it to Jesus. Along the way I'm calling out to Jesus, "Heal my friend, save my friend, touch my friend's life." My friend may not know Jesus today, but if they have an encounter with Jesus, I'm going to bet that they will leave Jesus riding their own wave.

I love how the friends' faith creates a wave of momentum that the paralyzed man rides to Jesus. Who in your life is far from Jesus? You may be their only friend who would rip through a roof for them. Take some time to pray for them today. As you pray, imagine tearing through a roof to get them to Jesus. May your moved heart move the heart of God, and create a wave of momentum for God to touch their life.

NOTES

WEEK SIX / DAY SIX & SEVEN

What idea was most challenging this week?

_____

_____

_____

_____

_____

_____

What day or concept do you want to rethink about?

_____

_____

_____

_____

_____

_____

WEEK SEVEN

WEEK SEVEN / DAY ONE

BOLDNESS AND FAITH- BOLDLY GOING WHERE NO MAN HAS GONE BEFORE

[24] "and the boat was already a considerable distance from land, buffeted by the waves because the wind was against it.
[25] Shortly before dawn Jesus went out to them, walking on the lake.
[26] When the disciples saw him walking on the lake, they were terrified. 'It's a ghost,' they said, and cried out in fear.
[27] But Jesus immediately said to them: 'Take courage! It is I. Don't be afraid.'
[28] 'Lord, if it's you,' Peter replied, 'tell me to come to you on the water'
[29] 'Come,' he said.
Then Peter got down out of the boat, walked on the water and came toward Jesus. [30] But when he saw the wind, he was afraid and, beginning to sink, cried out, 'Lord, save me!'
[31] Immediately Jesus reached out his hand and caught him. 'You of little faith,' he said, 'why did you doubt?'"

MATTHEW 14:24-31

L ast week my oldest daughter (Hailey) was on a mission trip in Idaho. She was there with a handful of students from the ministry school she attends. On one of their first days of the trip their team decided to go pray at the state capitol. Their assignment was simple: pray for the government and be open to the Lord's opportunities that He brings your way. So Hailey was walking around by herself and praying and eventually sat down on a bench outside the state capitol. A woman was sitting nearby and Hailey struck up a conversation. As they got to talking Hailey simply asked questions and listened. Now, Hailey didn't ask the normal "how are you doing/ what do you do?" questions, but more probing like, "what are your dreams, what are your fears?" type questions. Eventually the woman asked, "Who are you and what are you doing here?" Hailey shared with her that they were a group of students simply there to minister. The woman asked, "Do you have some time to come talk with me in my office?" Hailey responded with a yes. The woman led Hailey to the capitol building and inside, to a very nice (clearly high-class) office and they sat down. They spent the afternoon talking; Hailey listened and encouraged, they processed together, and Hailey prayed for her. The woman was not just any woman; she turned out to be one of Idaho's state Representatives. And Hailey had just spent the afternoon listening to, encouraging, and praying with her. At the end of the day the woman gave Hailey her cell phone number and said, "If there is anything you need while here in the state, just give me a call."

That night Hailey decided to take another bold step. She texted the Representative and said, "I don't know if you'd be open to this, but a small group from my team would love the opportunity to come and pray over you, your staff, the Governor if they are available, or anyone you'd like." The Representative quickly replied and invited Hailey to bring a team to do just that. The following day Hailey and some members from her team spent the day praying over some of the highest government leaders in Idaho. They were even invited to pray about a particular bill and invited into the chambers where that bill was on the floor being debated. The bill, if passed, would have legalized and funded pornography in libraries in the state as well as pornography in children's books. Thank the Lord the bill was denied! But Hailey said the best part was the government leaders who were praising God when the bill was denied and giving Him glory. They proceeded to thank Hailey and her team for all they had done and all their support.

I'm proud of Hailey in many ways. But I'm mostly proud of her willingness to take risks. I'm proud of her guts to take bold steps of faith. In a 48-hour period of time, there were a dozen bold moves she made to take her from one situation to the next. To take her from a bench, to an office, to the chambers where a bill was up for debate. This story wouldn't exist without the risks and bold steps of faith she took.

This week we are going to be focusing on taking bold steps of faith. Perhaps up until now, you've been stretching your faith in places no one would see. Maybe you've been contending behind closed doors for people and situations in ways you've never done before. Maybe God has been showing up in powerful ways as you're exercising different traits that grow your faith. But this week, we're going to be asking God to help us to take our faith from private to public. We're going to ask God to help us take steps of faith to places where it may be seen and stir conversation. This week we're talking about BOLD faith.

In our reading for today in Matthew 14, we visit a well-known encounter between Jesus, His disciples, and specifically an act of faith in Peter. This encounter happened immediately following the feeding of the 5,000. Jesus and His disciples have just experienced one of the most radical miracles to date. No one in their day had ever experienced the miraculous multiplying of food to feed a crowd like what had just taken place. Immediately Jesus sent His disciples in a boat to cross to the other side of the Sea of Galilee. But the wind picked up and they were caught out in the sea. And then Jesus does what He does: He goes walking out to them on the water.

As He approaches, He says to them, "Take courage! It is I. Don't be afraid." Peter immediately asks to walk out on the water to Jesus. What's interesting to me is that Jesus didn't throw the idea out there or suggest to all the disciples that they should consider walking on water. Nowhere does Jesus challenge them to do so. The place where Peter got the idea is Jesus himself and what He was modeling. Jesus is doing it, and Peter wants to do it as well.

I think most Christians are more like the other disciples. We are waiting for a clear invitation to try the scary, the impossible, or take the risk, as opposed to wanting to initiate our first step out of the boat, not because we were invited, or Jesus suggested it, but because Jesus is our model of walking on water.

Instead of sitting around and waiting for Jesus to say to us, "Have you considered taking a step of faith and walking on water?", we need to start taking our own step of faith knowing Jesus is already out there.

What's so insightful in this encounter is how Peter models both a high level of faith and then the losing of faith (at least to some degree).

We know how the story goes. Peter saw the wind and the waves, became afraid, and began to sink. Jesus comes to his rescue and then makes a statement, followed by a question.

"You of little faith," he said, "why did you doubt?"

You of little faith. That's interesting because Peter was just walking on water. I think most of us would say that is great faith. And I think Jesus would agree. But then when Peter's eyes focus away from Jesus and to the storm around him, he "loses faith" as doubt overcomes him. We could argue Peter displays great faith, and then displays losing his faith. (Not losing faith like he's walking away from Jesus forever, just losing faith in what Jesus could do for him in the moment). We go from living in the most amazing moment (walking on water) to the scariest moment (sinking in a storm) in seconds.

If there is anything we can learn from Peter in what he modeled, I would challenge us in two ways.

1. Take a BOLD step. Don't wait for the suggestion to walk on water. Take the bold step of faith to go where Jesus is already walking.

2. Lock eyes on Jesus. Keep your eyes fixed on Jesus and not the storm around you as you take the bold step of faith.

I grew up watching "Star Trek" with my dad. The original "Star Trek." That's right, William Shatner, Leonard Nimoy, and the rest of the original cast. I loved the tagline that every Trekkie knows and probably even those who didn't watch the show have heard: "To boldly go where no man has gone before."

That's what the whole show was about. It was about exploring new frontiers, strange new worlds, and seeking to go where no one else had ever gone.

Peter took a step of faith where no one else (besides Jesus) had ever gone before. Maybe for you, if you're the first Christian in your family, you may literally be going where no one else in your family has gone before. Every step feels risky and unknown. For others, to take a step of faith where no one else has led you may look like taking your faith into your workplace. You may feel like no one else is a Christian there, and no one else has taken this step of faith there before.

There are many times when our bold steps of faith will feel like we are the first people to go where no one else has gone before. That's okay. I will encourage you with the same words Jesus spoke to Peter. He says, "Take courage! It is I. Don't be afraid."

Go on, take a bold step out of the boat. Go where no man has gone before. You can do it! Jesus is waiting out there for you!

DAILY CHALLENGE: Have you been waiting in the boat for Jesus to make a suggestion of what you could do to take a bold step of faith? If so, why? If walking on water might represent taking a bold step of faith with Jesus, where might He be calling you to go? What might He be calling you to do? What are the wind and waves in your situation? What has a tendency to cause fear in you, cause doubt in you, and cause you to lose faith?

NOTES

WEEK SEVEN / DAY TWO

BOLDLY LIVING WITH NO FEAR OF MAN

³ "They seized Peter and John and, because it was evening, they put them in jail until the next day."

⁷ "They had Peter and John brought before them and began to question them: 'By what power or what name did you do this?'

⁸ Then Peter, filled with the Holy Spirit, said to them: 'Rulers and elders of the people! ⁹ If we are being called to account today for an act of kindness shown to a man who was lame and are being asked how he was healed,¹⁰ then know this, you and all the people of Israel: It is by the name of Jesus Christ of Nazareth, whom you crucified but whom God raised from the dead, that this man stands before you healed.'"

¹³ "When they saw the courage of Peter and John and realized that they were unschooled, ordinary men, they were astonished and they took note that these men had been with Jesus."

ACTS 4:3, 7-10, 13

¹⁸ "They arrested the apostles and put them in the public jail. ¹⁹ But during the night an angel of the Lord opened the doors of the jail and brought them out. ²⁰ 'Go, stand in the temple courts,' he said, 'and tell the people all about this new life.'

²¹ At daybreak they entered the temple courts, as they had been told, and began to teach the people."

ACTS 5:18-21

I remember one day when I was a young boy playing at a neighbor's house. We were hanging out in his garage talking, messing around and somehow we got to talking about Jesus. I wanted to tell him all that I (as an eight or nine year old kid) knew about Jesus. I told him about Jesus dying on the cross for our sins and Jesus wanting to be his Savior and friend. Then he asked me bluntly, "Can I invite Jesus to be my Savior now?"

Right as he asked, his dad walked into the garage. His dad was a gruff man. He was pretty rough around the edges, and I was always intimidated by him. As he walked in, he asked with a gruff, confronting tone in his voice, "What are you boys doing?" To which I replied, "Nothing." I locked eyes with the neighbor boy, my eyes glaring at him, trying my best to say "drop it" with my stare. He caught my vibe and dropped it.

It was a week later when we picked up the conversation and I did my best at that point to lead the boy to Jesus. But I remember feeling horrible all week. I remember feeling like I had missed the moment, all because of fear. I was afraid of his dad. I was afraid of what he would say to me. I was afraid what he might do if I was leading his kid in a direction he didn't want his kid to go. I let the fear of man stop me dead in my tracks.

This happens all the time in people's faith journeys. They want to share their testimony with someone but fear keeps them quiet. They want to pray out loud with their spouse but fear keeps them from praying. They want to talk about Jesus with their kids but the fear of looking like they don't know enough keeps them from trying. They want to get free from the enemy's stronghold in their life, but fear keeps them from facing it. They want the relationship to be restored but fear is keeping them from apologizing. They want to live boldly for Jesus but fear of "what people might think" keeps them from taking their next step of faith.

The fear of man is one of the biggest things that keeps Christ followers from living boldly in their faith. And today is the day we face it head on.

Today in our scripture reading we do a "fly-by" of Acts 4 and 5. To dive in further, read the entire chapters for yourself. But for our purposes, I wanted to highlight a few moments in these chapters. In Acts 3, the disciples, Peter and John, heal a man who had been crippled (lame) his whole life. This had caused a stir in Jerusalem as people wanted to hear from these two men who healed a lame man.

Peter and John start boldly proclaiming Christ. At the same time they are condemning the Pharisees and the religious leaders who had Christ crucified. This results in them being thrown in prison twice. They are in the crosshairs of the religious leaders of the day, but notice how they respond.

Acts 4:13 says, "When they saw the courage of Peter and John... ".

That's how these guys respond. They respond courageously. They respond boldly. They respond with no fear in the midst of this life-threatening situation.

I don't know how you or I would respond if we were thrown in prison for our faith. Would it cause us to take heed and pause? I'd like to think I would respond with even greater boldness, but I honestly don't know. The fear of man is a powerful thing. What others think about us is a powerful thing. But we have to get over it if we want to take bold steps of faith.

Consider these real-life situations that I've been in.

I'm standing by my fence in my yard talking to my neighbor. They are sharing a real-life crisis with me. I want to pray with them for what they are facing, but what will they think of me if I do?

I'm getting my oil changed. As I small-talk with the manager, they share a real-life crisis that the shop has recently faced. I want to pray with them, but what will they think of me if I do?

I'm in a grocery store. A worker starts chatting with me and shares how his wife is dying. I want to pray with him, but we are in public; what will people think, what will he think if I do?

I'm having breakfast with someone. They share a difficult life situation they are going through and I want to pray with them. But I know this requires a little longer prayer than a typical short one before a meal. We're going to be sitting at this table praying for quite some time if I start. Will this make the other person uncomfortable? Will it make the other diners uncomfortable?

I could go on and on about the many times I've felt like it's time to activate my faith, but immediately question, "what will people think?"

I did not overcome my fear of man every time. I'm thrilled that the fear of man doesn't hold me like it did in the past, but it has been a process of taking little bold steps one after another.

Getting past the fear of man doesn't come easy for anyone. But it is something we must embrace pushing past if we want to see our faith soar to new levels.

DAILY CHALLENGE: Where does the fear of man keep you from taking bold steps in your faith? Has the thought "what will people think" kept you from activating your faith in the past? Let's pray today that God will give you an opportunity to take a bold step of faith. When the thought pops in your head today, "what will people think," take that as an indicator that now is the time to move forward to take the risk. Come back and write down what opportunity the Lord placed before you today. Did you step into it boldly... partially... or not at all?

NOTES

....

....

....

....

....

....

WEEK SEVEN / DAY THREE

BOLDLY INITIATING

[1] "On the third day a wedding took place at Cana in Galilee. Jesus' mother was there, [2] and Jesus and his disciples had also been invited to the wedding. [3] When the wine was gone, Jesus' mother said to him, 'They have no more wine.'

[4] 'Woman, why do you involve me?' Jesus replied. 'My hour has not yet come.'

[5] His mother said to the servants, 'Do whatever he tells you.'

[6] Nearby stood six stone water jars, the kind used by the Jews for ceremonial washing, each holding from twenty to thirty gallons.

[7] Jesus said to the servants, 'Fill the jars with water'; so they filled them to the brim.

[8] Then he told them, 'Now draw some out and take it to the master of the banquet.'

They did so, [9] and the master of the banquet tasted the water that had been turned into wine."

JOHN 2:1-9A

I'm going to revisit one of those real-life scenarios I mentioned yesterday. I was in the produce section in the grocery store and one of the workers I often see was there. He is a very friendly older man who talks with every customer he sees. In my opinion he is the greatest asset in the entire store, not because of how hard he works, but because of how he makes everyone feel. A big box grocery store is usually not a place where you feel seen or known by anyone. But this guy breaks through all of those stereotypes. As we were chatting that day, he shared how his wife was really sick; she was dying. On top of that he was dealing with his own health issues.

Now I know we weren't in church. We weren't at a scheduled appointment. We were standing next to the bananas. I'm pretty sure I was in a hurry, as I am whenever I'm shopping. He was working. It wasn't what anyone would consider the "picture-perfect moment" to stop and pray. But that didn't stop me this time. I asked, "Would you mind if I prayed for you and your wife?" He welcomed it. I placed my hand on his shoulder right there in the produce section and prayed for healing for him and his wife. After I finished praying, he grabbed me and gave me a big hug.

That day, I stepped into a Kingdom opportunity. I'm grateful that I didn't miss it. I'm grateful that I decided to just go for it. Today we're considering the importance of boldly initiating. Often we just want the opportunities to come to us. And sometimes they will. **But often the greatest way to grow our faith is to NOT WAIT, but INITIATE.**

In John 2, we have the very first miracle that Jesus performs on record. How the miracle comes about is probably as fascinating as the miracle itself. The miracle is Jesus turning water into wine at a wedding banquet. But the way the miracle is initiated is worth diving into.

Check out what happens.
³ "When the wine was gone, Jesus' mother said to him, 'They have no more wine.'
⁴ 'Woman, why do you involve me?' Jesus replied. 'My hour has not yet come.'"

We could call Mary, the mother of Jesus, the very first believer. She is the very first person to have the Messiah identified to her. It will be her child who will be the Savior of the world. She knows it. And she's known it Jesus' entire life. So here they are, Jesus is 30 years old, he's starting to acquire a few followers because of the way he teaches scripture. But even they are skeptical followers. In fact, it is not until after this miracle that they really start to believe in Him. That's what it says in verse 11: "What Jesus did here in Cana of Galilee was the first of the signs through which he revealed his glory; and his disciples believed in him."

So He has followers, but no believers. He hasn't performed any miracles yet. But Mary comes to Him and says, "They have no more wine" (wink wink).

In other words, I believe in you, and I know you can do something about it.

Jesus replies, "My hour has not yet come." He knew once the miracles started, He would be on a straight trajectory into His ministry years and ultimately toward the cross. Additionally, one of the things we see Jesus talk about regularly is only doing the will of the Father and only doing the work of His Father. In this case, His earthly mother is trying to initiate something that His Heavenly Father has not yet impressed on His heart to do. And Jesus will only do what the Father says.

What this means is that **somewhere between what Mary initiated and Jesus performed, the Father affirmed.**

God the Father was moved by the faith of Mary in such a way that He would affirm her request for Jesus to perform the miracle.

And Jesus would respond by recognizing the voice of His Father and saying "Oh, now's the time."

If we learn anything from this first miracle, it is the importance of trying to initiate something in faith. I imagine God is delighted when His children try to initiate something on His behalf. I imagine God is moved at times, like with Mary, and affirms what is trying to be initiated.

Back to the grocery store. How do you think our Heavenly Father looked upon that situation when I was praying for miraculous healing in the middle of the produce aisle? Honestly, I don't know if He led me to the prayer, or I initiated the prayer. Either way, I ended up praying, so I guess it doesn't matter. But the model of Mary is to just go for it.

I never want to step outside the will of the Father. But how often do we miss an opportunity to exercise our faith boldly because we are waiting for clear direction? I didn't have a clear direction of what to do in the produce aisle. I just had a clear opportunity. That's what Mary had. She didn't have clear direction but she had an obvious and clear opportunity. And so she initiated.

What if every time we had a clear and obvious opportunity we just tried to initiate our faith? I imagine God would be moved by our faith more than we would imagine and we would see God do some amazing thing in and through us.

DAILY CHALLENGE: Today, look for an opportunity to boldly exercise your faith. Then, simply try to initiate something on behalf of God. Whether it is sharing something with another person, praying for someone, serving someone, or giving to someone, if there is a clear opportunity, step into it and see how God responds to your faith.

NOTES

WEEK SEVEN / DAY FOUR

BOLDLY OBEDIENT

[10] "In Damascus there was a disciple named Ananias. The Lord called to him in a vision, 'Ananias!'

'Yes, Lord,' he answered.

[11] The Lord told him, 'Go to the house of Judas on Straight Street and ask for a man from Tarsus named Saul, for he is praying. [12] In a vision he has seen a man named Ananias come and place his hands on him to restore his sight.'

[13] 'Lord,' Ananias answered, 'I have heard many reports about this man and all the harm he has done to your holy people in Jerusalem. [14] And he has come here with authority from the chief priests to arrest all who call on your name.'

[15] But the Lord said to Ananias, 'Go! This man is my chosen instrument to proclaim my name to the Gentiles and their kings and to the people of Israel.'"

ACTS 9:10-15

I've only had this happen to me one time in my 20+ years of ministry. I say that because I don't want you to think this is an everyday occurrence. Years ago there was a couple in my church who I knew had been struggling for years to get pregnant. When I say years, I'm talking like a decade of trying. So I was shocked and nervous when I felt the Lord impress something on my heart to pray over and say to the couple. I felt like the Lord was asking me to pray over them that they would become pregnant. Now that's fine with me. I have no problem asking God for miracles. But then I felt like the Lord wanted me to say something to them, specifically, a prophetic declaration over them. I felt like He was telling me to say to them, "Go home and prepare the nursery." I had this internal wrestling with the Lord, but I decided to boldly and obediently say what I felt the Lord was calling me to say. Well, almost nine months later to the day, that couple had a healthy and beautiful baby.

Boldly walking in obedience on that occasion felt really risky. Since then, the Lord regularly impresses things on my heart that I feel like I need to respond to in obedience. It's not just a matter of missing the opportunity, it's a matter of obedience to what God is asking of me.

Bold obedience is a powerful way to stretch and grow our faith.

In Acts 9, we see a man who is being called to respond to God in bold obedience. The man is Ananias. At this point in history, the disciples are spreading the Gospel everywhere they go. Ananias is a disciple of Christ living in Damascus. At this point the Apostle Paul is referred to as Saul and he is not yet a follower of Jesus. Saul has just had a life-altering moment with the resurrected Christ during his journey to Damascus. The Lord appeared to him in a bright light, spoke from heaven, then blinded him. He's been blind for three days, just thinking about that encounter with Jesus.

The Lord wants to use Ananias to restore Saul's sight and help him take his first steps into ministry. That's a pretty awesome assignment: to pray for someone knowing they will get their sight and help them start their journey with Jesus. But Saul is not just anyone. Saul, up until now, was the greatest religious leader in opposition to Christians. He was the one leading the charge to throw Christians in prison, persecute them, and even have them killed.

Of all the assignments from the Lord, this one may be one of the least appealing. What if Saul receives his sight and immediately picks up where he left off? He would arrest Ananias for sure, and maybe have him killed.

So it makes sense that Ananias is scared and hesitant. But Ananias boldly takes the step of obedience and is used by God just as God intended.

Want to know what the long-term impact was because of Ananias' obedience? It is the fact that we even know he existed. Do you realize if

Ananias hadn't obeyed God, we probably wouldn't know about him today? He probably wouldn't have made it into the Bible for anything else. So here we are, 2,000 years later, and we know of his life and the important role he played in the restoration of Paul's sight.

For you, walking boldly in obedience may not look like praying for an enemy. It may be something as simple as doing the right thing when no one else is.

Everyone else is bending the truth at work in one area, or lying about it. But you choose to boldly do the right thing and walk in obedience to God.

Everyone else is sleeping around. Other couples are living together. But you choose to do the right thing, to do the obedient thing.

Everyone else is gossiping. But you choose to do the right thing, to do the obedient thing.

Everyone else is... fill in the blank. But you choose to do the right thing, to do the obedient thing.

It may put your relationships at risk, your reputation at risk, your job status at risk, or your influence at risk. But these bold steps produce some of the greatest gains in our faith. So step boldly into obedience and watch God grow your faith through it.

DAILY CHALLENGE: How might doing the right (or obedient) thing be risky? Is there anything you know God has asked you to do that you haven't stepped into yet? Why haven't you? Today if God asks you to do something, obey boldly and see how He grows your faith.

NOTES

WEEK SEVEN / DAY FIVE

BOLDLY SPEAK

[16] "While Paul was waiting for them in Athens, he was greatly distressed to see that the city was full of idols. [17] So he reasoned in the synagogue with both Jews and God-fearing Greeks, as well as in the marketplace day by day with those who happened to be there. [18] A group of Epicurean and Stoic philosophers began to debate with him. Some of them asked, 'What is this babbler trying to say?' Others remarked, 'He seems to be advocating foreign gods.' They said this because Paul was preaching the good news about Jesus and the resurrection.
[19] Then they took him and brought him to a meeting of the Areopagus…"
[22] "Paul then stood up in the meeting of the Areopagus and said…"
ACTS 17:16-19A, 22A

Many years ago, I was working out at my local gym. It was an arm day and I was going through my normal workout routine. I grabbed some dumbbells and faced a mirror to start doing alternating curls. Right arm curl, left arm curl, right arm curl, left arm curl. During this routine, a man stepped right next to me, and while facing the same mirror, started curling in sync with me. It was completely random, but it was hilarious to see the two of us curling in sync with each other. If there was an Olympic sport called synchronized weight lifting, I think we would have dominated it. We both started laughing because we knew how silly it must have looked.

Our laughter turned to introductions and we started chatting. I asked about him, how long he had lived in the area, what he did, etc. I came to find out he had some kids, was divorced, was now in a new relationship and engaged to be married. I asked if working out was what he did for fun. He replied, "Oh it's just something to do. You know, life is life. You get up, go to work, go to the gym, go home, have some beers, watch some TV and do it again the next day."

Then he asked me, "What do you do?"

I told him, "I'm a pastor."

To which he looked at me bewildered and asked, "Why?"

I replied, "Well, because I believe there is so much more to life than getting up, going to work, going to the gym, going home, having some beer, watching TV and doing that over and over again."

His face shifted from bewildered to intrigued.

I continued to run into him at the gym and we'd talk about life, his upcoming engagement, parenting, as well as my church. A few weeks later, he, his fiancée, and his kids came walking into church on a Sunday morning. This continued, and a couple of months later when I was preaching, I gave an opportunity to respond to the gospel during our closing prayer. I asked people to simply look up at me and lock eyes with me if they wanted to give their life to Christ at that moment. I was floored when I looked over and both he and his fiancée were looking me straight in the eyes. That was a sweet day, all because I said something boldly that challenged his thinking.

In Acts 17, the Apostle Paul finds himself in the city of Athens. He is so distressed by the idol worship that is rampant in the city that he can't help himself: he has to go and speak boldly about Jesus day in and day out.

In our day and age, idol worship looks different, but in essence it is still the same thing. Worship means to ascribe worth. So idol worship is anything other than God that we ascribe great worth to. It's anything that gets our primary attention or is prioritized over God. When we put it in those terms our culture is filled with idol worship.

It's when people make work their greatest priority.

It's when people make their children their greatest priority.

It's when they make their kids' sports team their greatest priority.

It's when they make their stuff their greatest priority.

An idol could be your favorite TV show, your video games, your phone, your house, your car, your boat, your hobby, your food, your exercise, your clothes, your appearance, your power, your property, your knowledge, or whatever you prioritize over God.

The reason why I list all that is because it's everywhere, yet I don't know if we are as distressed by the idol worship in our day as Paul was distressed by it in his day. It disturbed him so much that he couldn't help but speak up and say something about it.

When it comes to growing our faith, sometimes the easiest way to grow it is to talk about it. When we boldly talk about our faith, we actually set ourselves up for God to use our testimony in powerful ways.

I wonder how many of us have stunted faith simply because we are quiet. We don't want to "preach" to people so we say nothing. Yet saying nothing to those who need Jesus may be one of the most unkind things to happen to the individual whose eternity lies in the balance.

Romans 10:14 says "How, then, can they call on the one they have not believed in? And how can they believe in the one of whom they have not heard? And how can they hear without someone preaching to them?"

Do you see it? How can they respond to the gospel if they haven't heard? It is our responsibility to share the truth of Jesus with those in our lives. If you want to see your faith stretched, start speaking boldly about who Christ is and what He has done in your life. You'll discover He will use you to help others discover faith while your faith grows.

DAILY CHALLENGE: What keeps you from speaking boldly about faith? Is there someone in your life that you think might be open to a conversation about Jesus? Let's pray that the Lord gives you an opportunity today or this week to speak boldly to them about your faith. Come back and journal how that went and what you learned. How did you feel your faith was growing or being stretched in the process?

NOTES

WEEK SEVEN / DAY SIX & SEVEN

DAY 6: LET THAT THOUGHT SIMMER

What idea was most challenging this week?

DAY 7: LET THAT THOUGHT SIMMER

What day or concept do you want to rethink about?

NOTES

WEEK EIGHT

WEEK EIGHT / DAY ONE

FAITH AND THE WORD: CAPTURING THOUGHTS

"Keep this Book of the Law always on your lips; meditate on it day and night, so that you may be careful to do everything written in it. Then you will be prosperous and successful."

JOSHUA 1:8

[3] "For though we live in the world, we do not wage war as the world does. [4] The weapons we fight with are not the weapons of the world. On the contrary, they have divine power to demolish strongholds. [5] We demolish arguments and every pretension that sets itself up against the knowledge of God, and we take captive every thought to make it obedient to Christ."

2 CORINTHIANS 10:3-5

Have you ever been a head case? You feel like you're having a wrestling match in your mind. And what you're wrestling with is your own thoughts.

We see this happen in sports all the time. One of the most globally shocking examples this was when Simone Biles pulled herself out of the 2020 Olympics. During her vault, the first event of the team final, Biles got lost in the air and didn't know where her body was in relation to the ground. She ended up performing a much simpler vault. When she landed she was clearly shaken. Biles immediately walked over to her coach and said she was not in the right "head space." After the event she said, "I have to focus on my mental health… It just sucks when you are fighting with your own head." (CNN Sports, 7/29/21)

Maybe you've felt like Simone at some point in your life. I know I have. All of us have wrestled with our thoughts and our thought patterns. What if I told you that learning to "think rightly" could be one of the most impactful aspects of growing your faith? The follow-up question becomes, "What do we use to direct our thinking?"

The answer to that and the focus for our week is: THE WORD OF GOD.

Using the Word of God to direct our thinking shapes our faith and directs our lives.

How do we go to war in our minds and end in victory?

The context surrounding Joshua 1:8 is this. Joshua is getting ready to go to war. Giants are in the land. The Israelites are heading into this place called the promised land and the first city they are facing is the well-fortified city of Jericho. Notice God's instructions about winning the battle they are about to face:

"Keep this Book of the Law always on your lips; meditate on it day and night, so that you may be careful to do everything written in it. Then you will be prosperous and successful."

While they are facing a literal battle, their instructions are the same instructions that we see throughout scripture for winning the battle in the mind. Keep the Word of God on your lips, in your mind, and obey it. This will give you the victory.

Learning how to use God's Word in our lives will help us win the battles we face. Over the next two days I want to give you two simple steps to win the battle of the mind with the Word of God.

The first step is to CAPTURE THE THOUGHT.

"We demolish arguments and every pretension that sets itself up against the knowledge of God, and we take captive every thought to make it obedient to Christ."
2 CORINTHIANS 10:5

You and I are going to have to learn how to grab hold of a thought and make it obedient to Christ. That's a fascinating concept and we'll come right back to it, but first, what are the thoughts that we need to grab hold of?

The word that gets translated as "arguments" is the Greek word *logesmos*.

It can be translated as arguments, imaginations or reckonings. I like "imaginations" because that translation helps me quickly identify thoughts that need to be captured. How often do you imagine the worst? How often does your fear feed off of imagining the worst?

Years ago, my son smashed his hand and we were afraid he had broken multiple bones. We took him to Urgent Care where he got an X-ray. It turned out he didn't have any breaks, praise God. However, the X-ray did reveal a dark spot that appeared to be in the middle of a bone in his finger. The radiologist caught it and had some concern. The next thing we knew they referred us to an oncologist at Children's Hospital. What? Why? Did they think our son had bone cancer? As you can imagine, the weeks that followed were weeks where it was difficult not to imagine the worst.

We are pretty good at imagining the worst. Have you ever lost sleep over fear, anxiety, or imagining something that never came to be? You probably have. Lisa and I lost a lot of sleep during those weeks with my son. While it ended up being cartilage in the bone and really no big deal, our imaginations got the best of us. Or maybe I should say, brought out the worst in us.

So what do we do with those imaginations?

We take them captive.

One of the things I like to do is personify my fears, my anxious thoughts, my imaginations, or the lies I believe. I imagine a person wearing a t-shirt with the word on the t-shirt that represents what I need to take captive.

Let's imagine my fear is not being able to financially provide for my family. I imagine someone wearing a t-shirt that says "provision" or "$$$." I literally imagine grabbing the individual and putting them in a jail cell. As I place them in the cell I ask God to help me understand why that thing is causing me fear. What's the root cause? Is it my own control, my own insecurities, is it misplaced values, is it because I have some idols in my life?

As I ask these questions, God starts to show me where I've made this fear bigger, stronger, more intimidating than it is. He shows me where my perspectives are off or where I'm rehearsing thoughts that war against God's promises.

How about you? Where are you a head case?

Today is the day to start winning the war in your mind. We're going to use the Word of God and the principles in the Word of God to win this battle. As you do so, you'll find your faith being strengthened, stretched, and encouraged. Let's get after it: let's take some things captive today.

DAILY CHALLENGE: Where are you a head case? Where do you have a tendency to imagine the worst? If you had to personify your fears, what words are on the t-shirt? Ask God to help show you the root cause of that fear: is it your own control, insecurities, misplaced values, or an idol in your life? Today in faith, we are declaring that these things being taken captive will not continue to rule our minds.

NOTES

WEEK EIGHT / DAY TWO

FAITH AND THE WORD: CORRECTING THOUGHTS

"Keep this Book of the Law always on your lips; meditate on it day and night, so that you may be careful to do everything written in it. Then you will be prosperous and successful."

JOSHUA 1:8

"We demolish arguments and every pretension that sets itself up against the knowledge of God, and we take captive every thought to make it obedient to Christ."

2 CORINTHIANS 10:5

I grew up in a family who loved playing games. It was pretty normal to hear someone ask almost every night, "Do you want to play a game?" Whether it was a card game, a board game, a strategy game, a partner's game, or an individual game, I was usually up for it.

Now, here's the big question: did your parents go easy on you when playing these games?

I know parents who are as ruthless when playing with their kids as they are with other adults. And then there are those parents who take it easy on the kids. They let some things slide. They allow some "house rules" into play.

That second description is how I play as a parent with my kids. I'm probably a little too lenient at times because sometimes I know my kids are just making up more "house rules" on the spot to try to get an advantage.

Once we were playing Sorry! and my kids got out of control making up "house rules" the entire time. They would say, "we play this way..." and then say something that made no sense, or clearly gave them an advantage. Eventually I got fed up with them and called them out on it and said, "Those aren't the rules and you know it."

I decided at that moment that I wouldn't let the kids keep making me follow rules that didn't apply to me.

Similarly, the enemy (Satan) does the same thing with us all the time. When it comes to spiritual dynamics, the enemy has to follow the spiritual rules. So what does he do? He wants to keep you from knowing the rules or enforcing the rules. He will constantly try to make up rules that play to his advantage and if you don't correct the enemy because you don't know the rules, he'll get away with it.

Yesterday we talked about capturing thoughts. Today we take it to the second step and that is to CORRECT THE THOUGHTS.

The second half of 2 Corinthians 10:5 says, "we take captive every thought to make it obedient to Christ."

To make something obedient to Christ is to hold it up to Christ until we see it as He sees it. Scripture talks about the fact that we can know and have the mind of Christ. Wouldn't you like to know exactly what Jesus thinks about some of the things you think about? That's what making it obedient to Christ is all about.

I've said it this way before: **I can't afford to have a thought in my mind about me or my situation that He doesn't have in His mind about me or my situation.**

So what I do is I personify the things I'm facing. We talked about that yesterday. I capture it, then I CORRECT the thought by telling it the rules according to scripture. I look into scripture to see what it says about what I'm facing. I ask, "Jesus, what do you think about this? What are the rules of your kingdom regarding this?"

The reason why we need to know what scripture says and what Jesus thinks is because to make something obedient, we have to know the rules.

Let's say the enemy is telling you the lie that you will always live in fear. It might sound like this in your mind: "Not everyone can be super courageous and you're just a fearful person. You'll probably always struggle with fear."

The problem is, that statement is a lie and it goes against what the spiritual rules say about the children of God.

2 Timothy 1:7 says, "For God has not given us a spirit of fear, but of power and of love and of a sound mind." (NKJV)

To correct the thought is to speak and enforce the rules over whatever you've captured.

We need to, in faith, declare the Word of God and its rules to our situation. In this case I would remind my heart and mind what is true about me, and that is that God has not given me a spirit of fear. God has given me a spirit of power, love and a sound mind.

You have to tell your finances the rules.
You have to tell your insecurities the rules.
You have to tell your shame the rules.
You have to tell your anger the rules.
You have to tell your offense and lack of forgiveness the rules.
You have to tell the lies you've been believing the rules.

Joshua 1:8 reminds us to meditate on the truth (the spiritual rules of God's Kingdom) day and night. That Hebrew word for mediate is *haiga*, which can also be translated as muse, or imagine. Yesterday we talked about how in 2 Corinthians 10:5 the word "argument" can also be translated as "imaginations."

So here we have two different ways we can imagine in scripture. Instead of imagining the worst, we choose to imagine the Word of God being effective in our lives.

Another way of saying it is, we capture every ungodly imagination and choose to replace it with godly imagination.

I want to imagine the truth of God's Word being effective in my life day and night.

Imagination will destroy you if you live in the imaginations that come up against the knowledge of God. Imaginations will free you if you live in the imaginations of the truth of God.

Who is lording over your imagination?

Let's revisit the situation with my son's finger from yesterday. We had just gotten a call from the doctor's office referring us to an oncologist. How many of us would naturally start to imagine the worst? How many of us would naturally start to imagine the storyline of God showing His power and the spot is miraculously gone, or healed, or God faithfully providing peace throughout the journey, or God providing the perfect set of doctors and medicine to bring about complete healing? Or, as it ended up being, not anything worth worrying about at all.

We don't often imagine the victorious God story. We have a tendency to imagine the worst story.

But what we need to start doing is imagine the truth from God's Word being effective in your life and in your situation. Imagine the victories God will provide and the way He will meet your practical, emotional, and spiritual needs. We need to start marinating our thoughts and our mind in the Word of God.

I like the imagery of a marinade. You marinate a hunk of meat in a sauce so that the meat takes on the flavor of the marinade. In the same way, we need to marinate our minds in scripture so that our minds take on the flavor of the Word of God; our minds take on the flavor of heaven and the rules of heaven.

DAILY CHALLENGE: What thought did you capture yesterday? How will you correct that thought today? You may want to pick a subject or do a word study in the Bible. Find one verse that speaks to whatever subject you are dealing with. Meditate (marinate) on a verse: imagine it, memorize it, turn it over and over and over in your mind. What rules of God's Kingdom does it teach you? In faith, declare the new rules over your life and your situation.

NOTES

WEEK EIGHT / DAY THREE

FAITH AND THE WORD: SPEAKING THE WORD

"The tongue has the power of life and death,
and those who love it will eat its fruit."

PROVERBS 18:21

"Keep this Book of the Law always on your lips; meditate on it day and night, so that you may be careful to do everything written in it. Then you will be prosperous and successful."

JOSHUA 1:8

"A good man brings good things out of the good stored up in his heart, and an evil man brings evil things out of the evil stored up in his heart. For the mouth speaks what the heart is full of."

LUKE 6:45

One year my son came home from camp and told us that he no longer liked oatmeal. When I made him oatmeal the day he returned home he replied, "Eww, gross, it's like vomit." This response was kind of a big deal because at that time, most of our kids ate oatmeal almost every morning. It had been his "go-to" breakfast and he had always loved it. So what changed? What caused a complete shift in his perspective toward oatmeal? What had happened is he had gotten himself oatmeal one morning at camp and all the boys at his table started talking about how it looked like vomit. They must have overdone it (as young boys often do) because that perspective was locked into his mind.

What's fascinating is how quickly he took hold of what he heard.

The same is true in us. Our hearts have the tendency to take hold of that which we hear. Words, once spoken, carry power. Sometimes that power is just perception or a perspective, like my son's new perception/perspective of oatmeal, but it is powerful all the same.

I don't know what's been spoken over you, maybe a lie like one of these statements:

You're not going to succeed.

Why do you even bother trying?

You're a liar.

No one likes you.

You'll never beat that sin.

You'll always be a spiritual baby.

You can't stand up to the devil alone.

You'll always be alone.

You'll never have a true friend.

These words have power.

This is how Proverbs 18:21 describes the power of our words: "The tongue has the power of life and death." It is describing how the power of life and death can exist within our tongue, our words.

Have you ever had someone come up to you and say something that hurt you to your core? We might even say "it was like being stabbed in the heart" to describe moments like these. That's how painful words can be. They kill. They carry the power of death.

Conversely, have you ever had someone come up to you and give you a compliment that seemed to change your entire perspective for the day? All of a sudden you were floating on cloud nine. You were happier. You were encouraged. You were energized. That's because words also carry the power of life.

Consider these two phrases: "You can't do anything great." Vs. "Anything you do can be great."

You can just hear death and life in those phrases.

Here's another way Proverbs 12:18 puts it, "There is one who speaks rashly like the thrusts of a sword, But the tongue of the wise brings healing." (NASB)

This is why it is so important that we learn to speak the Word of God. As we speak it, it impacts perception and perspectives and aligns our thoughts with God.

Joshua 1:8 tells us to "Keep this Book of the Law always on your lips."

We know there is real power in speaking the truths from God's Word over your life. Now Joshua instructs us how often we should keep these thoughts in front of us: always. There is a need to constantly be speaking the truth over our lives. We really can't get lazy in this area. It doesn't work well if you think you can speak some truth once a week over your heart and keep it on track.

Maybe you've heard the stat saying that it takes 10 positive statements to neutralize one negative statement in your life. **If you think you can renew your mind in truth just one day a week while it's being bombarded by lies of the enemies the rest of the week, you're sorely mistaken.**

God knows that this endeavor is a daily endeavor. We need to speak life, truth, and God's Word over our lives daily.

Finally, speaking the Word is connected to our faith.

Romans 10:17 says, "faith comes by hearing, and hearing by the word of God." (NKJV)

Don't miss this. Faith is initiated by hearing. You can't hear something if it's not (spoken) declared. Meaning, you need to hear DECLARED what God says (what Christ's perspective is). This actually initiates and grows faith.

There are many amazing byproducts of speaking the Word of God. There is the power of life, there is truth, there is insight, there is wisdom, but on top of all that there is growth for our faith.

So speak the Word out loud. Speak life. Speak it daily!

DAILY CHALLENGE: Your words carry the power of life and death. Let's make it our aim today to only have words that "speak life" come out of our mouths. Is there someone in your life who you know desperately needs the Word of God spoken over them today? Do it! Be the one who speaks life over them. We, too, need the Word spoken over us. What verse do you need to speak over yourself today?

NOTES

WEEK EIGHT / DAY FOUR

FAITH AND THE WORD: PERSPECTIVE AND DIRECTIVE

[1] "'In those days and at that time,
when I restore the fortunes of Judah and Jerusalem,
[2] I will gather all nations
and bring them down to the Valley of Jehoshaphat.
There I will put them on trial
for what they did to my inheritance, my people Israel,
because they scattered my people among the nations
and divided up my land.'"

JOEL 3:1-2

[9] "Proclaim this among the nations:
Prepare for war!
Rouse the warriors!
Let all the fighting men draw near and attack.
[10] Beat your plowshares into swords
and your pruning hooks into spears.
Let the weakling say,
'I am strong!'"

JOEL 3:9-10

One of my favorite SNL ("Saturday Night Live") characters was Stuart Smalley. The skits that showcased him were called "Daily Affirmation with Stuart Smalley." His tagline was the best, as he would stare into a mirror and say to himself, "I'm good enough, I'm smart enough, and doggone it, people like me." Each skit was filled with ridiculous words of affirmation and encouragement, which they always took over-the-top, but that of course was the point.

While it may have seemed silly, there was actually a shadow of a Biblical principle buried in those skits. It was the declaration of a right or good attitude over an individual, even prior to them carrying the attitude.

We actually see this in scripture as a powerful tool in our faith journey. **It's declaring something true even when you don't see it.**

In the book of Joel, Judah and Jerusalem have been conquered by Tyre and Sidon, and God wants to free them from this slavery they've been caught in. So the prophet Joel gathers the people of God together and brings a message to them.

There are two things from within this message in Joel that I think we can learn in terms of speaking the Word and how it helps grow our faith.

The first is embracing God's PERSPECTIVE.

In verse one he communicates God's perspective of their situation. It's interesting what God sees. "In those days and at that time, when I restore the fortunes of Judah and Jerusalem."

Do you see God's perspective? God sees a restoration of the fortunes of Judah and Jerusalem. That perspective would have been difficult for anyone else to even imagine. The people of Israel have been slaves for years. They have no land. They have been scattered among the nations. They lack leadership. They lack community. They lack unity. They are outgunned and outmanned. Yet God sees them as on the verge of the restoration of their fortunes.

The first thing we must do is embrace God's perspective.

Years ago Lisa and I were house hunting. We had lived in Wisconsin for over a year. We had rented a house which we had maxed out. It was a three bedroom, two bath home and we were a family of nine. To say we were on top of each other was an understatement. So we looked and we looked for a house. Nothing seemed to be a good fit for us. Then all of sudden a pretty sweet opportunity came before us. It was a large home with plenty of space. But it was also an older home with a lot of work to be done, it would have required us to move to another nearby town, maybe have our kids switch schools, and increase our driving distance to church. We prayed about it and we felt like the Lord said, "Not this one, I've got a better one for you."

So we reluctantly walked away from it. We wondered if we were doing the right thing. You see, at this point, we had been looking for months and there was nothing on the market in our price range that would meet our needs.

We felt like God's perspective was that He had something better for us. But if I'm honest, I couldn't see it at all. Whatever the "better" was, it wasn't on the market.

It's really difficult to embrace a perspective that seems impossible or at least improbable. For weeks I wondered if we had made the wrong call. But then, one day, out of the blue, we got a phone call. A house had become available. It was "completely unexpected" even from the homeowner's perspective. The family who was living there suddenly needed to move and this home that was literally the perfect home for us just came to us.

Do you think any of that took God by surprise? Of course not. He always had the perspective that the perfect house provision would come to us. We simply struggled to see it and it seemed impossible, or at least improbable. Yet choosing to embrace His perspective even when we don't see it is that first step for us.

The second step is a DIRECTIVE. That directive is to start responding to God's perspective and speak God's perspective.

In Joel 3:9-10 it says:

"⁹ Proclaim this among the nations:
Prepare for war!
Rouse the warriors!
Let all the fighting men draw near and attack.
¹⁰ Beat your plowshares into swords
and your pruning hooks into spears.
Let the weakling say,
'I am strong!'"

Notice what he tells them to do. Beat your plowshares into swords and your pruning hooks into spears. In other words, start responding to God's perspective. Start preparing to step into God's perspective. Start living like you're going to experience God's perspective. For them it meant that although they had no military or military leader, they should prepare for war.

For us in our home situation, what that meant was that we literally started preparing to move even when nothing was on the horizon. We started going through our stuff and purging the extra items we had accumulated. It seemed a bit crazy to start prepping to move when there was nothing to move to, but that's what it means to respond to His perspective.

Along with that, Joel says, "Let the weakling say, 'I am strong!'"

That's a pretty crazy directive, to speak out loud something that you are not. But in this case, the weakling is declaring how God actually sees them.

Our words when declaring God's perspective and God's truth possess God's power. They bring about God's kingdom perspective. There is something divine and supernatural in declaring what God sees.

I know you may not see it, but there is something faith-filled in embracing God's perspective and declaring it over yourself today.

Here are some kingdom perspectives you may want to declare over yourself today.
I carry life in my words.
I am courageous.
I am strong.
I am loved.
I carry ALL the fruit of the Spirit.
I have an abundance of grace for today.
I will not be shaken.
…and the list could go on and on.

DAILY CHALLENGE: As you think about perspective and directive, what is God's perspective over a situation you are facing today? What directive would He give you to take a step toward His perspective today? Is there a kingdom perspective in the list above or another one that is not listed, that you need to declare over yourself today?

NOTES

WEEK EIGHT / DAY FIVE

FAITH AND THE WORD: BECOMING PROCLAIMERS

[7] "How beautiful on the mountains
are the feet of those who bring good news,
who proclaim peace,
who bring good tidings,
who proclaim salvation,
who say to Zion,
'Your God reigns!'
[8] Listen! Your watchmen lift up their voices;
together they shout for joy.
When the LORD returns to Zion,
they will see it with their own eyes.
[9] Burst into songs of joy together,
you ruins of Jerusalem,
for the LORD has comforted his people,
he has redeemed Jerusalem."

ISAIAH 52:7-9

I remember feeling a level of sadness and frustration when I heard my daughter flippantly say, "We are the worst class at school." I asked her what she was talking about. She said, "Oh, yeah, all the teachers hate my class, the kids in my class are horrible."

I was sad because she said it as if it were a well-known fact. I was frustrated because she and the rest of her class seemed to embrace it. I knew a lot of the students. There were plenty of good kids in her class who could have stood up to that mindset, determined to be different. But they weren't standing up to it, they were embracing it. In many ways it became a self-fulfilling prophecy. If you declare something over and over, it will usually come to be. That's because there is the power of life and death in our words.

Today as we continue looking at the power of God's Word and how it impacts our faith, we're focusing on the power of proclaiming.

In Isaiah 52, we see this idea of proclaiming/bringing/saying/shouting throughout the passage. Look at it again.

⁷ "How beautiful on the mountains
are the feet of those who bring good news,
who proclaim peace,
who bring good tidings,
who proclaim salvation,
who say to Zion,
'Your God reigns!'
⁸ Listen! Your watchmen lift up their voices;
together they shout for joy.
When the LORD returns to Zion,
they will see it with their own eyes.
⁹ Burst into songs of joy together,
you ruins of Jerusalem,
for the LORD has comforted his people,
he has redeemed Jerusalem."

The passage is saturated with the idea of proclamation. There is something supernatural about proclaiming something prior to its arrival.

We know it is prior to the arrival because of the state of Jerusalem. Verse nine describes Jerusalem as being in ruins. If a town is in ruins, you wouldn't think there would be shouts of joy, or people bursting into songs of joy. Yet that is what they are doing.

People are proclaiming good news, peace, good tidings, salvation, joy and that God is reigning.

What's amazing is that last statement: God is reigning. In fact they are to "say to Zion, 'Your God reigns!'" I can imagine that would have been really difficult to say since they were being ruled by another king and another nation. It probably didn't feel like God was reigning at all. But He was, and that is the point.

For us, it may seem as if God is losing in many ways around the globe. The coronavirus is still hanging on in some places. War is raging overseas. Government leaders are in constant conflict. Inflation is skyrocketing. Racial tensions are still strong in our country. Politics are more polarizing now than ever. Addictions are increasing. Church attendance is decreasing. People seem to fight about everything. And yet, OUR GOD REIGNS!

Are you catching this? OUR GOD REIGNS!

Because our words carry the power of life and death we need to become a people who start to proclaim that which is true even when we don't see it.

We need to become the people of God who proclaim:
- good news
- peace
- good tidings
- salvation
- joy
- and our God reigns

We need to proclaim His perspective.

Don't forget the enemy is speaking lies, he is accusing, and he's declaring as much death as possible. But that's all it is; he's speaking of a possibility. That means that there is another possibility. The other possibility is the kingdom of God coming and impacting a person, an area, or a situation. We need to be a people who will proclaim His truth. In doing so, we set up our situation to experience His truth.

We don't pretend to boss God around, but we do declare IN FAITH His promises, His nature, His ways, His kingdom rules, the power of the cross, and what the Word of God says.

The following is a prayer I wrote years ago. I've prayed it over myself hundreds of times. It's a prayer that proclaims His Word and His perspective even when I don't see it.

DAILY CHALLENGE: For your daily challenge today take some time to declare this over yourself.

My Father is King and I am His child. (Eph. 1:5)

As His child, I am royalty. (Eph. 1:18)

As royalty my inheritance is in heaven.

I am made for every heavenly reality.

I am made for abundance. (John 10:10)

I am made for significance. (Eph. 2:10)

I am made for impact.

I am made for purpose.

I am made to make disciples. (Matt. 28:19)

I am made to storm the gates of hell and set prisoners free by the power of the gospel. (Romans 8:21)

I am made for power. (Eph. 1:19-20)

I am made for resurrection work and resurrection prayers… prayers of such substance that they make God sweat. (Eph. 1:20)

My faith, although the size of a mustard seed, will move mountains. (Matt 17:20)

My Father fears nothing, so I will fear nothing. (2 Tim. 1:7)

My Father's will is perfect, so I will embrace today with its imperfections and difficulties knowing that greater is He within me, than he that is in the world. (1 John 4:4)

And while God has made me for great things, I will exist and live for His glory and His alone. (Phil. 2:11)

My Father in heaven,

may Your name be kept holy,

Your kingdom come,

Your will be done,

On earth as it is in heaven.

Give me this day my daily bread.

And forgive me my sins,

as I forgive those who sin against me.

Lead me not into temptation,

but deliver me from evil.

For Yours is the kingdom,

and the power, and the glory,

for ever and ever and ever and ever and ever and ever and ever.

Amen. (Matt. 6:9-13)

WEEK EIGHT / DAY SIX & SEVEN

DAY 6: LET THAT THOUGHT SIMMER

What idea was most challenging this week?

DAY 7: LET THAT THOUGHT SIMMER

What day or concept do you want to rethink about?

WEEK NINE

WEEK NINE / DAY ONE

FAITH, OBEDIENCE AND GAINING TRACTION: OBEDIENCE- WHY BOTHER?

"Keep this Book of the Law always on your lips; meditate on it day and night, so that you may be careful to do everything written in it. Then you will be prosperous and successful."

JOSHUA 1:8

My seven-year-old son is already showing signs of being a fairly typical male, specifically in the area of his inability to respond when in front of electronics. If he's playing a video game or watching TV, it doesn't matter what you say to him, it goes in one ear and out the other. He may have good intentions of being attentive, but he's just lost in his own world. What's funny is that he has acquired the correct response to us as parents during these occasions. We will be calling to him to get ready for bed, and if he's in front of electronics he'll respond with an appropriate, "Okay, I'm coming." But he then proceeds to sit there mesmerized in front of the TV, and doesn't take any steps toward obeying.

We'll come into the living room a few minutes later to see him still sitting in front of the TV. This time we'll say his name with greater conviction: "Brooks! It's time to get ready for bed." Without missing a beat he'll respond with, "Okay, I'm coming." But once again he won't move. He's good at saying one thing but then doing another.

Unfortunately, the same is often true in many of our faith journeys. We say one thing and then do another. God is calling us to obedience in an area of our lives that would strongly impact our faith journey. We respond to Him during a Sunday morning service and give Him lip service by saying, "Okay, God I'm coming," but then we don't follow through Monday through Saturday.

In Joshua 1:8, God instructs the children of Israel in this way regarding His Word. He says, keep it on your lips, meditate (think) on it, and be careful to DO EVERYTHING written in it.

Last week we focused the entire week on the power of the Word of God, how to interact with it and use it in growing our faith. This week we take it to that final aspect in Joshua 1:8 in how obedience and doing what the Word says will grow our faith.

How is "doing what the Word says" connected to success in our faith journey?
For the same reasons that:
- not just talking about a diet, but actually dieting makes all the difference.
- not just talking about exercise, but actually exercising makes all the difference.
- not just talking about learning a new skill, but practicing the new skill brings about the skill.
- not just saying to my wife, "I'm romantic"… but actually doing romantic things makes me romantic.
- AND not just knowing the Word of God and talking about it, but DOING it actually grows our faith.

We can't just be theorists of God's Word. Instead we must become doers of God's Word.

In fact, I believe everything in God's Word is to drive us to an experience of it. For example, there are over 2,300 Bible verses about money. They include topics like wealth, possessions, greed, money mindsets, contentment, investing, and more. They also commonly drive home the point that God is our provider. Now all of those verses are not just there for us to theorize about, but they are also there for us to experience. They invite us on a journey to not just believe that God CAN provide, but that God IS MY provider.

What does "doing" do?

When I say "doing," I'm talking about obedience.

Obedience always produces something. And that something is connected to our faith. Consider some of the following IF and THEN statements in scripture.

"...so that you may keep the law of the LORD your God. ¹³ Then you will have success if you are careful to observe the decrees and laws that the LORD gave Moses for Israel."

1 CHRONICLES 22:12B, 13A

"If you are willing and obedient, [then] you will eat the good things of the land;"

ISAIAH 1:19

"[if] My son, do not forget my teaching,
but keep my commands in your heart,
² [then] for they will prolong your life many years
and bring you peace and prosperity."

PROVERBS 3:1

"If you fully obey the LORD your God and carefully follow all his commands I give you today, [then] the LORD your God will set you high above all the nations on earth. ² All these blessings will come on you and accompany you if you obey the LORD your God:"

DEUT. 28:1-2

"But [if] whoever looks intently into the perfect law that gives freedom, and continues in it—not forgetting what they have heard, but doing it—[then] they will be blessed in what they do."

JAMES 1:25

Obedience always produces something. Every. Single. Time.

1 Chronicles says you will have success.
Isaiah says you will eat good things in the land.
Proverbs says you will prolong your life and have peace and prosperity.
Deuteronomy says God will set you high above.
James says it gives freedom and you will be blessed in what you do.

The point is obvious. Obedience to God's Word has a profound tangible effect on our lives. And every time someone experiences these outcomes, their faith grows and is further solidified.

My prayer for you and me is that we are not the children of God who are living such distracted lives that when God is calling us to do something we respond by saying, "Okay, I'm coming" but then never move. May we be a people who are not just hearers of the Word but doers also.

DAILY CHALLENGE: Is there an area in your life where you've heard the Word, but just haven't followed through in obedience yet? Why is that? Maybe it requires a stretching of your faith. Did you ever think that your step of obedience could create your greatest momentum in faith?

Tell someone a step of obedience you'd like to take this week.

NOTES

WEEK NINE / DAY TWO

FAITH, OBEDIENCE AND GAINING TRACTION: BREAKING BAD

[14] "but each person is tempted when they are dragged away by their own evil desire and enticed. [15] Then, after desire has conceived, it gives birth to sin; and sin, when it is full-grown, gives birth to death."

JAMES 1:14-15

Have you ever seen the movie "Groundhog Day"? Bill Murray plays a cynical TV weatherman who finds himself reliving the same day over and over again. He begins by taking advantage of different aspects throughout his repetitive day, but eventually he gets to the point where he tries to bring about the best that he can during his 24-hour period of time. Each day he finds himself "coming up short" in what he's trying to accomplish. He is then on the merry-go-round for another ride doing the same thing day after day after day.

Maybe you feel that way in your faith journey with God. Maybe your groundhog day is the story of the prodigal son. That story is awesome. But we are not meant to relive it day after day.

If you find yourself on the merry-go-round of following Jesus, falling into the same sin trap, confessing your sin, repeating the cycle (follow, fall, confess, repeat) we've got to talk through how to gain traction in this thing called obedience. There is nothing more maddening to one's psyche than repeating these defeated patterns in our lives.

Take it from one who knows. I've been there. And there's a lot of self-hatred, feelings of hypocrisy, personal anger, and frustration living that groundhog day over and over again. For the rest of this week we are going to look at principles that will help us get off that merry-go-round.

If you're not currently riding on the merry-go-round that I'm referring to, don't skip this week, for two reasons. One, if you're not riding it now, take notes for when you accidentally find yourself hopping on it in some form or fashion. I say some form or fashion, because sometimes the merry-go-round is as simple as an incorrect thought pattern. It's a lie that takes root in our thinking. Even something as simple as that will need to be broken. Second, there is likely someone close to you in your life that is on the merry-go-round. Pay attention this week so you can come alongside and help them hop off. So whether you're on the merry-go-round and want to get off, taking notes for the future, or coming alongside someone, there are some solid principles for us to put into practice to grow our faith.

The first principle that I would have us consider for this week is: Breaking Bad.

What I mean by that is, break the bad patterns that you find yourself caught in.

James describes a pattern that we often take toward sin which ultimately leads to our downfall. It starts with temptation and being enticed by our own evil desires. If we allow these desires to lead to sinful actions, sin continues to grow and eventually leads to death.

The point is, there is a pattern that leads us to sin. Very rarely do we ever find ourselves walking obediently with God and then moments later walking in complete disobedience to God. It doesn't happen that way, at least not usually. The more common merry-go-round we find ourselves on is one that is riddled with unhealthy patterns or habits in our lives that lead us to temptation, which leads us to sin, which leads us to a complete downfall.

So here's what I challenge you to do. Walk back your sin. Walk back the lie or the unhealthy mindset that you fall into. Walk it backwards and look for the pattern in your life.

Let's say the thing you struggle with is explosive anger. One doesn't usually go from happy one moment to exploding the next. There is usually a pattern. Before you exploded, you started yelling. Before you started yelling, you felt threatened. Before you felt threatened, you were feeling overwhelmed. Before you were overwhelmed, you were feeling agitated. Before you were agitated, you got caught off guard by something that someone said. Before you were caught off guard, you were happy. But you weren't just happy; when did it happen, how were you physically? Oh... it happened (and happens) in the evening after a long day, when you were worn down and tired.

So the start in breaking bad is actually to identify your pattern into your fall. Then when you identify the typical first step toward your fall, you insert a new pattern there. So consider our example of explosive anger. The first aspect was realizing your emotional and physical state. The explosions usually happen when you are worn down and tired. Start by noting that condition. Whenever you are worn down and tired, be on guard for the triggers that can set you on a trajectory toward your downfall. Second, insert a new habit in the pattern. Now when someone says something that catches you off guard, instead of getting agitated, insert something new. In this case, if it were me, I would insert the habit of quoting a verse. The verse could be about patience, taking thoughts captive, offering grace, whatever speaks to your issue. I find it's pretty difficult to sin when quoting scripture.

What you'll discover is that you'll cut the bad pattern off at the pass. You'll never make it to overwhelmed, threatened, or yelling because you broke the bad pattern early.

What is your pattern toward sin? What habits lead you toward an unhealthy thought or lie that derails your faith?

My wife will regularly warn me about my news consumption. I feel like it's important for me to stay up-to-date on current events. But she's right; consuming news can discourage me. The news can belittle my faith. The news has a tendency to rob me of believing big. It's small things like that which can become the habits in our lives that derail our faith.

Today is the day of breaking bad. It's a great day to break the bad habits in our lives and create new, healthy ones.

DAILY CHALLENGE: Pick one thing in your life that you don't like where it leads you. For example, a sin that traps, a lie, a thought pattern, or simply something that robs your faith, etc. Now walk it back. What's the typical pattern that you follow to get to that spot? Is there a new healthy habit you can insert in your pattern? Tell someone about your new habit and have them ask you about how you implemented it.

NOTES

WEEK NINE / DAY THREE

FAITH, OBEDIENCE AND GAINING TRACTION: AN UNHEALTHY VIEW OF GRACE AND MERCY

"What shall we say, then? Shall we go on sinning so that grace may increase? [2] By no means! We are those who have died to sin; how can we live in it any longer?"

ROMANS 6:1-2

"But whoever looks intently into the perfect law that gives freedom, and continues in it—not forgetting what they have heard, but doing it— they will be blessed in what they do."

JAMES 1:25

My kids are pretty gracious to one another. Sometimes they are too gracious. I know, you may be thinking, can someone be too gracious, too kind, too merciful? Yes, if the end result is actually to the detriment of the other sibling. Let me give you an example. Let's say two siblings are playing together. Child A is playing with a toy and Child B comes up and takes the toy from their sibling. It was clearly a selfish and unkind thing for Child B to do. I, as the parent, witness the stealing of the toy. I say to Child B, "You need to return the toy to your sibling and say you're sorry." Child A speaks up and says, "It's okay, they can have it."

Now, if Child A genuinely doesn't want to play with the toy anymore, that's fine, they can hand it to Child B. However, Child B must first hand the toy back to Child A and apologize, otherwise Child B is getting away with bad behavior and learning a very unhealthy way of life. They are learning that they can steal and get away with it. They are learning that if the other person offers them grace and mercy, then their actions are okay. And that's not true. Just because grace and mercy were offered, it doesn't make their behavior acceptable.

The same happens in Christian circles all the time. We offer grace and mercy where God isn't.

If we want to help others gain traction in their faith, we cannot offer mercy where God does not. Similarly, if we want to gain traction in our own faith we need to make sure we are not ignorantly pretending that God is offering us mercy where he is not.

In Romans 6 the Apostle Paul asks, "Shall we go on sinning so that grace may increase?"

What he is sarcastically asking is, should we sin more so that we can experience more of God's grace? Well, that's ridiculous. But some have actually bought that lie. Our youth director told me about overhearing some students on a retreat talking that way about sin. They said, "Well, that's the point of the cross, so we can sin however we want." That's not the point of the cross at all. The point of the cross was to make a way for us to be restored to a love relationship with God. In any love relationship, it wouldn't make any sense to say to that other person, "I love you," then go and do something that demonstrates the opposite.

God will always offer us grace and mercy, but that offer doesn't exist as a license to sin. It's a license toward a relationship. And that would be one sick and twisted relationship if that grace was offered simply so we could continue to wound the one who offered it.

An unhealthy view of God's grace and mercy is to show it where He doesn't.

Sometimes we think we are doing favors for God by showing people mercy. But what we are actually doing is insulating them from Gods' conviction. We end up protecting people from God's very sharp sword (God's Word is referred to as the sword of the Spirit) that is trying to bring healing and deliverance. To protect someone from the Holy Spirit's conviction is to protect them from the very freedom God wants to bring them; it shows mercy where God doesn't. An unhealthy view and application of mercy will keep others (or ourselves) thinking we are "all good" with God without having to obey Him.

For example, let's say a couple is living together before marriage. They claim to be Christ-followers, but they are acting like their living situation is okay in the sight of God. No one else is calling them out on their behavior. I find myself caught in this situation regularly in this day and age. But it doesn't change the fact that I still end up having to call the couple out and call them to obedience. To not do so is to insulate them from the blessings and freedom that God wants to bring them that is only found in obedience.

This was also happening in the early church in Corinth. The Apostle Paul addresses it in 1 Corinthians 5. Paul gets word of a man who is sleeping with his father's wife (his stepmom). The church is priding themselves with how much grace they are offering to this individual who is living in sin. Paul rebukes the entire church and tells them they should have expelled this immoral brother from among them. Offering this individual such grace was actually insulating him from God's conviction and the opportunity for him to turn from his sin, repent, and be made right with God again.

There is a reason why Jesus said to people who had been living in sin "go and sin no more." Because He knew, just like it says in James 1:25, that obedience brings freedom.

We get a restored relationship with God through faith in Jesus… that's grace. But we get freedom through obedience.

For us, He's always a God of grace and mercy. But never walking in obedience will forfeit the promises and blessings that God wants to pour out over you. It will also forfeit the ability for you to become the person God had in mind for you to be. It will forfeit the freedom you can have in Christ.

DAILY CHALLENGE: How about you? Are you offering grace and mercy to others where God isn't? Is there a Christ-follower who you are relationally close to, who you know is walking in sin and no one has called them out? Pray for an opportunity to have an honest conversation with them about what obedience can look like and the freedom it can bring to them.

Personally, are you embracing an unhealthy view of mercy? Is there any place in your life where you've told yourself that your sin is "no big deal" while God is calling you to obedience?

This obedience will grow your faith in profound ways… step into it today.

NOTES

WEEK NINE / DAY FOUR

FAITH, OBEDIENCE AND GAINING TRACTION: DON'T OPT FOR EASY

"¹³ Enter through the narrow gate. For wide is the gate and broad is the road that leads to destruction, and many enter through it. ¹⁴ But small is the gate and narrow the road that leads to life, and only a few find it.'"

MATTHEW 7:13-14

We were among the thousands, if not millions, of disappointed buyers one Christmas in the late 90's. A cutting edge, revolutionary new exercise gadget was hitting the market. It promised a flat stomach and washboard abs all while sitting back and doing nothing. "Let the Ab Flexer do the work for you," said the advertisement. The Ab Flexer was a belt you wrapped around your core. Once turned on, it would send electrical shocks into your ab muscles. While it touted many different levels of intensity (shocks) and many different programs, the programs all seemed the same and it felt like there were only two levels of intensity. Either barely-any-shock-at-all or curl-you-into-a-fetal-position shock. After about 10 minutes of this self-inflicted pain we came to the same conclusion that most everyone else did: that we had just wasted our money and we still had two more payments of $29.99 before we owned this piece of nostalgic exercise equipment.

We fell prey to the advertisements because who doesn't want great results without putting in great effort? We instinctively want things to be easy.

The truth is, when it comes to walking in obedience to God's Word, the world is offering easier alternatives in every direction. We often trade our eternal profit and pleasure (which is what is produced from obedience) for momentary profit and pleasure.

In Matthew 7, Jesus is describing the gate to eternal life. He describes it as a narrow gate that leads to life. While He's talking about faith in Christ, the same principle is actually true when it comes to following the Word of God as well. Walking in obedience to God's Word will often be a lonely journey. The world (culture) is walking a wide path with many alternatives to God's Word that is often a lot easier to walk.

Sometimes obedience can seem scary, especially when you are the only one doing it. You think to yourself, "I'll be the only one," "I'll stick out," or "People will think I'm crazy." That is sometimes the case when it comes to obedience. The sooner you embrace that you're on a narrow path, the better off you'll be.

Can you imagine Joshua addressing the nation of Israel as they are getting ready to face their very first opposition in the Promised Land? They come up against the well-fortified city of Jericho and God gives Joshua his marching orders. And the orders are just that–it's a lot of marching. God tells them to march around the city every day for six days straight in complete silence. Then on day seven, they are to march around the city seven times. After the final lap around the city, at Joshua's signal, the people of Israel are to shout. That's right, SHOUT. So the plan is walking and shouting. Can you imagine being Israel and hearing this plan? Can you imagine how insane it sounded? Can you imagine how crazy they looked in the eyes of their enemies?

Yet, they walked the narrow path of obedience and this battle that the Lord wins for them becomes a landmark battle for them. This battle strikes fear in every nation in the Promised Land. This battle becomes what Israel will look to when they need encouragement and point to when they are questioning and doubting.

When it comes to why we struggle with obedience, a key aspect is that we often opt for what is easy.

We have to fight this urge and embrace what is sometimes a difficult and narrow journey.

I wish the path to obedience was as simple as strapping on the Ab Flexer. But it's not. It's a path riddled with preaching scripture to yourself, accountability with friends, honest assessments of your behavior, time in God's Word, and time in prayer. While it may not be the easiest, it is the most life-giving, freedom-filled journey you can go on.

Today, don't opt for the easy way–opt for the narrow way that leads to life.

DAILY CHALLENGE: Obedience always leads to greater growth in our faith. Today consider where you've opted for easy. Is there something you're doing, "because everyone's doing it?" Is there some place you're going, some way you're spending, something you're watching or listening to, because everyone else is doing it? What's the narrow path of obedience that you're being called to walk?

NOTES

WEEK NINE / DAY FIVE

FAITH, OBEDIENCE AND GAINING TRACTION: BUILD A STRATEGY

"Keep this Book of the Law always on your lips; meditate on it day and night, so that you may be careful to do everything written in it. Then you will be prosperous and successful."

JOSHUA 1:8

"Blessed is the one
who does not walk in step with the wicked
or stand in the way that sinners take
or sit in the company of mockers,
² but whose delight is in the law of the LORD,
and who meditates on his law day and night.
³ That person is like a tree planted by streams of water,
which yields its fruit in season
and whose leaf does not wither—
whatever they do prospers."

PSALMS 1:1-3

I eat a gluten-free diet. I don't do it because it's trendy or naturally keeps me from eating garbage. I do it because quite a few people in my family have celiac disease. We all react differently to digestive issues, from pain to inflammation. The latter is what I deal with. I won't die if I have gluten, but I'll know if I eat any because I'll feel it in my knees later that day; I'll be walking like an old man by evening. There are a few occasions when it seems worth it to break my diet. Some desserts just seem worth it. But the older I've gotten, the fewer those occasions seem to be.

When I was younger I would often aim to be "mostly gluten-free." My problem was when I was "mostly gluten-free," I found myself eating more gluten than non-gluten foods. I would break my diet constantly. I had no real strategy other than to "try to limit my gluten." And when I had no rock solid strategy for success, I had no success at all. I discovered I had to limit all gluten to be successful.

I think there are many Christians who want to be "mostly Christian" in the same way that I wanted to be "mostly gluten-free." They want the Bible and obedience to it to be the primary thing in their lives, but they lack a strategy. Since their primary goal is to simply be "mostly obedient," they end up not hitting their goal more often than they would like.

To be successful in walking obediently to God's Word, we need a strategy to get us there. We need to build a plan toward success. Throughout this week, we've already touched on a handful of simple principles to walk in obedience, but today let's nail down some solid, yet simple, steps that should be a part of your strategy toward obedience.

Over the past couple weeks we've referenced Joshua 1:8. In that verse we've got two solid steps in our walk toward obedience. We've already hit on these, so I will just mention them.

1. Speak God's Word. Regularly practice declaring God's Word over your life as well as in the face of temptation when it comes your way.

2. Meditate on God's Word. Remind your heart and mind of what scripture says regarding who God says you are and what He says about the temptation that comes against you.

Read Psalm 1:1-3 for these next three steps.

3. Look who you are walking with.

Verse one says, "Blessed is the one who does not walk in step with the wicked."

I don't know if you've heard this statement before, but I've seen it to be true in people's lives. "You are the average of the five people you hang around with most." Simply meaning, **whoever you hang out with most you will end up acting like, thinking like, behaving like, and being like.**

I picture this like a three-legged race. Remember those from back in elementary school? You stand side by side with someone and tie your legs that are closest to each other together. Then you run a race tied to your partner. You can't help but work toward walking in step with each other.

In Psalm 1, the author is warning us of purposefully tying ourselves to others who are walking wickedly. It's foolish to purposely keep up with or build friendships with people who will lead us astray. You will end up walking in step with them into wicked ways. Take a good hard look at those you are walking with. Instead of walking with the wicked, we can purposefully build relationships with others who will encourage our faith and push us forward.

4. Look where you are standing.

Verse one goes on to challenge us to not "stand in the way that sinners take."

This is challenging us to **make sure not to position ourselves in a place where we know temptation is coming.** You know where temptation often comes against you. It's when you are alone in that place. It's when you go to that friend's house. It's when you linger at work or meander at the gym. It's when you go to the coffee house or the bar.

In Psalm 1, it's described as purposefully going to a place where you know temptation is coming. If we want to walk in obedience we need to do the opposite. We build a strategy that takes us away from temptation. We make sure not to go where we know sin is waiting to have us.

5. Look where you are sitting.

Verse one finishes by warning us not to "sit in the company of mockers."

In other words, **be ready to get up and leave.** In the verse, he's warning them about being stationary. Don't stay in a place if temptation comes there. Part of our strategy should be to be prepared to escape situations that turn south.

The beauty is that to escape stationary people, all you have to do is leave. We've all been in a conversation that turned into gossip. What should you do then? Leave. Or, it's the party that turned into "that kind of party." It's the movie that took a turn for the worse and you know you shouldn't stay.

I've left all of those situations at some point in my life. I've left the group conversation, the movie theater, the concert, the party, the hangout, the "whatever" that took a turn. Be prepared, make it a part of your strategy, and be ready to leave.

DAILY CHALLENGE: Let's not just hope we become more obedient to God, let's build a strategy of obedience. As you consider these five different steps you could take in building your strategy, what steps do you think you need to implement immediately? Which steps will be the most difficult for you? Build a strategy today and share the key steps in your strategy with a trusted friend.

NOTES

WEEK NINE / DAY SIX & SEVEN

DAY 6: LET THAT THOUGHT SIMMER

What idea was most challenging this week?

DAY 7: LET THAT THOUGHT SIMMER

What day or concept do you want to rethink about?

NOTES

WEEK TEN

WEEK TEN / DAY ONE

FAITH AND FINANCES:
OUR TREASURE REVEALS OUR HEART

[19] "'Do not store up for yourselves treasures on earth, where moths and vermin destroy, and where thieves break in and steal. [20] But store up for yourselves treasures in heaven, where moths and vermin do not destroy, and where thieves do not break in and steal. [21] For where your treasure is, there your heart will be also.'"

MATTHEW 6:19-21

Years ago, one of my children asked me why I had to work so hard. They said, "Why don't you just go to that machine that gives you money and get whatever cash you want?" They were referring to the ATM machine. I laughed and explained to them that it didn't quite work that way.

Wouldn't that be nice if money issues were that simple? Wouldn't it be great if we could just go to a machine and get the cash we needed? Unfortunately, that's not reality and money seems to have a greater impact upon us than we would like. If deciding between a love or hate relationship with money, most in our culture probably lean toward the hate side of it. I say this because of the financial burden most carry. Consider these money stats:

- Total U.S. credit card debt is over $800 billion. That's nearly $3,000 per person in the U.S.
- There are 1.9 billion open credit cards in the U.S. That's more than 10 per person.
- Millennials have a savings rate of -2%, thanks to factors like high student loan debt and the skyrocketing cost of living.
- Nearly 70% of those divorced point to money as their top reason for divorce, ahead of infidelity.
- The phrase "how to budget" receives 72,102 unique searches on YouTube every month.

The truth is we all need it, we all have to spend it, we all have to earn it, we all have to learn how to save it, we all have to learn to budget for it, and we all have to learn where to say yes to it and where to say no to it. We can be wise with it, foolish with it, and generous with it. It can cause stress and laughter, sorrow and joy. It can consume your mind and have your heart. It's a subject that Jesus spoke about more than any other subject in scripture, which tells me that money is deeply connected to our faith journey. In fact, there are few things that can grow your faith faster than how you engage with God and your money.

This week, go "all in" on the faith experiment, and trust God to new degrees with your money. Get ready for Him to show up in powerful ways and watch your faith grow.

In Matthew 6, as Jesus is talking about money, He gives some simple insights about how money impacts us. For now, let's start at the end: that is, let's start at the end of Jesus' statement. He ends with a powerful exclamation point of a statement as He says, "Where your treasure is, there your heart will be also."

What Jesus is saying is, above everything else in this world, what you treasure will reveal what really has your heart. I would even say we could reverse it: where your heart is, there you'll find your treasure invested. Because wherever your heart is, your time, talent, and treasure will follow.

When Lisa and I were first dating, this principle was easily seen in my life. While I'm a pretty frugal guy, I was more than happy to spend my money on a nice date, a gift, a meal, going to a show, etc. I didn't think twice about investing my earthly treasure in the woman who had my heart.

I think we can interchange which comes first, treasure or heart. The point is, wherever you find one, the other will be tagging along.

To challenge you, consider this statement. Wherever your money is will reveal what you love most.

Maybe a good question is: What does your bank account reveal you love most? Most of us want to ignore that hard question and just continue living life, maybe because our money reveals something about our hearts that we are not proud of.

If you're a Christian, I believe you naturally want to love God with all your heart, soul, and mind. But that's easier said than done. If you want to put that statement to the test, then we have to learn how to trust God with our finances. And **it's not because God wants your money, it's because God wants your heart.**

Additionally, take notice in Matthew 6:20 that God is not anti-treasure. In fact, it actually appears like God is "pro-treasure" and for us having it. He's just most concerned about having treasure in the right place.

He says, "'But store up for yourselves treasures in heaven, where moths and vermin do not destroy, and where thieves do not break in and steal.'"

He actually wants our hearts to store something up for the end. In this passage God gives us a command. Sometimes we don't like commands, but this command almost sounds funny to us. God is saying, do whatever you can to store up, to acquire wealth or treasures in my Kingdom.

So how do we do that?

Check out what 1 Corinthians 3:8-15 says.
[8] "The one who plants and the one who waters have one purpose, and they will each be rewarded according to their own labor. [9] For we are co-workers in God's service..."
[12] "If anyone builds on this foundation [the gospel] using gold, silver, costly stones, wood, hay or straw, [13] their work will be shown for what it is, because the Day will bring it to light. It will be revealed with fire, and the fire will test the quality of each person's work. [14] If what has been built survives, the builder will receive a reward. [15] If it is burned up, the builder will suffer loss but yet will be saved—even though only as one escaping through the flames.
I CORINTHIANS 3:8-9A, 12-15

In this passage, we are the co-workers in God's service. Our work (what we do with our time/talents/treasures) will be tested to see if it was built with kingdom materials.

Are you aware that you can spend your life not participating in God's purposes for you? You can invest your time, talents and treasure for an end that will not last, and when it is tested it will be consumed by fire.

What will last through the fire? It's not just money that is used for kingdom purposes, it's every obedient step of faith you took this side of heaven, from the smallest word of encouragement you felt the Lord told you to say to someone else, to the greatest sacrificial gift you gave to the Lord. Everything you've done in obedience to God is building something that carries eternal wealth to the END.

But it's not about the money… it's all about the heart. So what does your money say about your heart?

DAILY CHALLENGE: What does your bank account reveal about your heart? Have you considered how you might be able to use your earthly treasure to store up treasure in heaven? What could that look like for you today? Is there an area in your finances that you feel like God is asking you to trust Him with?

NOTES

WEEK TEN / DAY TWO

FAITH AND FINANCES: SET OUR HEARTS ON THE RIGHT TREASURE HUNT

[21] "'For where your treasure is, there your heart will be also.

[22] 'The eye is the lamp of the body. If your eyes are healthy, your whole body will be full of light. [23] But if your eyes are unhealthy, your whole body will be full of darkness. If then the light within you is darkness, how great is that darkness!

[24] 'No one can serve two masters. Either you will hate the one and love the other, or you will be devoted to the one and despise the other. You cannot serve both God and money.'"

MATTHEW 6:21-24

Years ago Lisa and I were involved in a multi-level marketing business. While I don't oppose these businesses as a whole, I have realized they are not for me, mainly because as a pastor I have a primary call upon my life to make disciples of Jesus, not to make it to the next level in a business. But for our brief stint in the business there was a common motivating tool that was used. They would say something like, "What's your dream house, car, vacation? Cut out a picture of that and put it on your refrigerator. Then every single day that you walk past that picture, remind yourself what you're chasing after. Look at it and use it as a motivator to ask the next person, to make the next call, to go to the next meeting…"

I'm not against setting goals and creating self-motivating tools in one's life. But in this case, their focus was always to fix your eyes on things. The motivator was always stuff-oriented which is ultimately money-oriented. The answer to every problem in those businesses seemed to be answered with "more money."

You'll find that it's difficult to not let the things of this world take hold of your heart if you're constantly fixated on the things of this world.

Today we continue diving into the subject of money and your heart. In Matthew 6:21, Jesus makes a powerhouse statement: "wherever your treasure is, there your heart will be also." Then He immediately makes some cryptic statements about your eyes being the lamp of your body and the light being darkness within you.

What is He saying and what does He mean?

When Jesus says, "The eye is the lamp of the body," He means whatever you look at, focus on or fixate on, shines something upon your heart. And when He says, "If then the light within you is darkness," He's saying your eyes (your focus) can be fixated on earthly treasures, and if you do so you're actually shining dark things over your heart.

Picture it this way: every spring I hop on the same emotional rollercoaster. Nice weather arrives, and with it all the motorcycles start coming out. I've owned three motorcycles over the years. All of them were when I was much younger. And when I sold my last one it was to pay for some family expenses. When I sold it, my wife said to me, "Well, you know you'll have another one some day." I replied, "I will?" And she said, "Of course!" Those words have rattled around in my head for the past 20 years since I sold my last bike. I've always wondered when that next bike will come. But with nine kids and a home there is always a more pressing financial need. The want of a motorcycle is very low on my priority list. But without fail, every spring, I can't help but start looking for motorcycles. I look online to see what's available. And you'll never believe it: there is always something available. There is always a good deal out there somewhere. There is always a motorcycle that looks appealing to me and perfect for me.

My problem is that the more I look, the more discontented I am. The more frustrated I find myself in "not having."

It's interesting to me, because all winter it's not a temptation to me. It's only once I start looking that I start living in discontentment.

Proverbs 14:30 says "A heart at peace gives life to the body, but envy rots the bones."

That's exactly what happens when I fixate on what I don't have. It creates this ongoing envy that rots away within me. There is an aching within my soul and I know it's a reflection of jealousy and envy.

This is what Jesus was warning us about when He finished talking about treasures and then immediately connected it to our eyes and how they shine something on our hearts.

Since the eyes are a lamp to the body, it will shine something on the heart. The follow-up question is, what type of treasure hunt are my eyes sending my heart on? Are my eyes sending my heart on a treasure hunt for "earthly treasure" or for "kingdom treasure"?

Here's a simple way to redirect your eyes and what you're looking for.

Take $20 and set it aside to be used by God as He would direct you. Then keep your eyes open for a kingdom assignment. He might impress on your heart to pay for another car in the drive thru, pay for someone's groceries, get someone a gift, buy some supplies and make a meal for someone, or simply to give it away to someone in need. But in doing so, you're setting your heart on a different type of treasure hunt. Instead of fixing your eyes on things in <u>this</u> world, you're fixing your eyes on an assignment from <u>His</u> world.

DAILY CHALLENGE: What have your eyes been shining on your heart? Have your eyes been fixated on things that are breeding discontentment and envy? How can you send your heart on a hunt today that will store up treasures in heaven? Consider taking up the $20 challenge. Look for how God would have you use this "small treasure" for His purposes.

NOTES

WEEK TEN / DAY THREE

FAITH AND FINANCES: HEALTHY HABITS

"Go to the ant, you sluggard;
consider its ways and be wise!
[7] It has no commander,
no overseer or ruler,
[8] yet it stores its provisions in summer
and gathers its food at harvest."

PROVERBS 6:6-8

My younger kids are not good at saving money. They are probably like most kids; as soon as they have a dollar they want to spend it. It's funny to me, because there will be times that they want something that costs maybe $10, but they struggle to even be able to save that much because they can't help but spend the dollars as they come in one at a time: $1 here on gum, $1 there on cotton candy, and so on. They just don't have good habits associated with their money yet. Unfortunately, many adults struggle to grow out of some of these bad habits that were formed in our younger years.

Proverbs 6:6-8 points to the ant as an example of one who has simple, yet strategic, habits that build healthy provisions for the future. Today I want to do a quick overview of some basic healthy habits that apply to our money. Money experts have touted these same principles, but the truth is they were good Biblical principles and habits before they were good cultural principles and habits.

Consider where you are at and how you are doing with the **5 Biblical Healthy Financial Habits.**

1. Spend less than you earn.

It sounds simple enough, yet most of us struggle with it. Many who struggle with their finances actually think the answer is to just "make more money." But I would argue you can live within your means TODAY. If you can't learn to do it today, you will probably still be struggling with this in the future.

It's not an income issue, it's a spending issue.

Do you know what these pop stars all have in common?
50 Cent
Kim Basinger
MC Hammer
Mickey Rooney
Meatloaf
Stephen Baldwin
Elton John
Toni Braxton
Michael Jackson

They all went bankrupt. It's not that they lacked money. They lacked discipline in their spending.

Ecclesiastes 5:10 says, "Whoever loves money never has enough; whoever loves wealth is never satisfied with their income."

Can I translate that for you? Whoever spends more than they earn will never earn enough.

2.   Avoid the use of debt

"The rich rule over the poor,
and the borrower is slave to the lender."
PROVERBS. 22:7

When you owe a payment every month you feel like a slave to that payment. With the exception of your house payment (which most Christian financial counselors consider acceptable debt), make it your goal to limit the number of monthly payments you make.

This is becoming more and more difficult as businesses are becoming monthly payment businesses. Subscription-based business has taken over in recent years. I know how difficult this is, yet each of your monthly subscriptions are like little slave masters over you. So do what you can to limit monthly subscriptions and avoid all debt if possible.

Make a list of every monthly payment you're currently making. Are there any that you can pay off? Are there any subscriptions you can get rid of? Eliminate, eliminate, eliminate.

3. Build Margin (Save)

"The wise store up choice food and olive oil,
but fools gulp theirs down."
PROVERBS 21:20

Every financial counselor will tell you to build an emergency fund. $1,000 is a bare minimum in this day and age. There is nothing more stressful in life than when a crisis comes and you've got nothing saved for that day.

A few years ago a hail storm swept through our area and pounded our neighborhood. Our house got really beat up. We had significant roof and siding damage. Even with our cedar siding there were entire boards missing chunks of wood from the storm. Luckily insurance kicked in and helped with all the repairs. However, even with insurance, we had some of out-of-pocket expenses. I was grateful on that day that we had literally "saved for a rainy day."

4. Set long-term goals

"A wise man thinks ahead; a fool doesn't and even brags about it!"
PROVERBS 13:16 (TLB)

"Go to the ant, you sluggard;
consider its ways and be wise!
7 It has no commander,
no overseer or ruler,
8 yet it stores its provisions in summer
and gathers its food at harvest."
PROVERBS 6:6-8

You've probably heard it said, "When you aim at nothing, you hit it every time". That's so true when it comes to your finances. If you don't set saving for investment goals, you'll probably find that you have no problem spending what you make. You may be unpleasantly surprised when you realize, too late, that you are not ready for retirement or a financial emergency.

The proverb is teaching that we need to set some goals that take us into the next season. And that we, who are wiser than an ant, can plan financially for the next season we will be facing.

With nine kids, Lisa and I have faced some significant financial expenses. Kids are just expensive. And as they get older, they get more expensive. Their clothing is more expensive, feeding them is more expensive, cars, driving, insurance, college, etc., it's all expensive.

This year we will have three kids in college and our aim is to help provide some financial support for each child each year they are in school. While kids going off to college feels like it comes out of nowhere, the truth is it doesn't sneak up on you without warning. You can see it coming, and you know exactly when it will likely arrive. With this in mind, Lisa and I started saving little by little years before our kids hit their college years. We wanted to have habits in place long before our kids got there that would support our goals. But that's the point. We had some long-term goals, and so our spending habits were impacted early on by our goals.

5. Give

"Remember this: Whoever sows sparingly will also reap sparingly, and whoever sows generously will also reap generously. [7] Each of you should give what you have decided in your heart to give, not reluctantly or under compulsion, for God loves a cheerful giver."
2 CORINTHIANS 9:6-7

I've never met a Christian who doesn't want to be generous. It's hard-wired into us because our God is a generous God. However, there are far too many Christ-followers not following the model of Christ in living generous lives. Many are not living it because they haven't implemented Biblical strategic habits and thus feel strapped in their finances.

If you're thinking to yourself, "I can't give until_____," I'm not trying to be rude, but I don't buy it. I've been there. And this is not to brag, but Lisa and I have always practiced Biblical giving even in our poorest seasons of life, and we've had some seasons where we were REALLY POOR.

Generosity is not driven by income. It's a matter of the heart and a matter of obedience. **What you'll find is that if you do your portion of trusting Him with your giving, He'll do His portion of providing for your needs.**

You can do this! You can practice all five of these healthy Biblical habits today. Let's get started!

DAILY CHALLENGE: Of these five habits, what habit do you feel strongest in? Which do you feel weakest in or most intimidated by? What step is God calling you to take into one of these habits? How is your faith being stretched in trusting God with your finances?

NOTES

WEEK TEN / DAY FOUR

FAITH AND FINANCES:
ENGAGING BIBLICAL GENEROSITY, PART 1

"'Bring the whole tithe into the storehouse, that there may be food in my house. Test me in this,' says the LORD Almighty, 'and see if I will not throw open the floodgates of heaven and pour out so much blessing that there will not be room enough to store it.'"

MALACHI 3:10

"All the Israelite men and women who were willing brought to the LORD freewill offerings for all the work the LORD through Moses had commanded them to do."

EXODUS 35:29

If you could have either a relationship with Jesus or $100 million, which would you choose?

Now... not which one DID you choose, but which one did you WANT to choose?

I know, it's kind of an unfair question. But it gets to our hearts' greatest treasure really quickly. Because money will always be trying to draw our hearts away from Jesus, we have to become purposeful to master our money so it doesn't master us. We have to put money in its rightful place on a regular basis. In choosing to practice Biblical habits and Biblical generosity, we remind our hearts who we are choosing to trust and we remind ourselves where our money belongs in our priorities.

In scripture there are 2,350 verses on finances and possessions. When we break down all these verses we see principles of stewardship as well as different types of giving.

When considering principles of stewardship, here are some of the principles we see:

1. **Principle of Ownership:** we don't own anything, He owns everything.

2. **Principle of Responsibility:** God has graciously entrusted us with the care, development, and enjoyment of everything He owns.

3. **Principle of Accountability:** each of us will be held accountable for how we stewarded what He entrusted us with.

4. **Principle of Reward:** we will receive eternal rewards according to how we stewarded what He entrusted us with.

Over the next two days we're going to focus our attention on the different types of giving we see in scripture. Today we will zero in on two of them.

The first is: **The Tithe**
Tithe literally means tenth.

Malachi 3:8-11 says:
8 "'Will a mere mortal rob God? Yet you rob me.
But you ask, "How are we robbing you?"
In tithes and offerings. 9 You are under a curse—your whole nation—because you are robbing me. 10 Bring the whole tithe into the storehouse, that there may be food in my house. Test me in this,' says the LORD Almighty, 'and see if I will not throw open the floodgates of heaven and pour out so much blessing that there will not be room enough to store it. 11 I will prevent pests from devouring your crops, and the vines in your fields will not drop their fruit before it is ripe,' says the LORD Almighty."

Here in Malachi, he calls out the people and says they are "robbing God" by not bringing their tithes to the Lord. It's also one place in scripture where God literally dares them to test Him in this. He says, "Test me in this and see if I will not throw open the floodgates of heaven... "

This has been one area where I have unashamedly challenged people to test God. I believe so wholehearted in His promise to take care of our needs, that this is the best test (experiment) you could ever step into.

While Malachi is in the Old Testament, we see Jesus affirm the tithe in the New Testament in Matthew 23:23 when he says, "'Woe to you, teachers of the law and Pharisees, you hypocrites! You give a tenth of your spices— mint, dill and cumin. But you have neglected the more important matters of the law—justice, mercy and faithfulness. You should have practiced the latter, without neglecting the former.'"

Here Jesus says we should practice the tithe, while not neglecting some of the greater matters of the law.

In 1 Corinthians 16:1-2 we see the early church model tithing; giving their first, giving their best, and practicing percentage-based giving. All these elements are reinforced as we practice the tithe.

How is tithing connected to our faith? I've often referred to the tithe as our tangible trust. There is nothing more tangible than putting our money where our mouth is. We don't just say with our lips, "God, I trust you," but the tithe helps us say it with our wallets as well. And when we do so, it reinforces what we say with our lips. It reinforces our trust in Him.

When it comes to the tithe, **our motivation** is trust and obedience. And **God's response** to it is to meet our every need, pour out blessings (open the flood gates of heaven), and provide protection (rebuke the devourer).

The second type of giving we see is: **First Fruits and Offerings**

This is giving that goes above and beyond the tithe.

In Deuteronomy 26:1-10 we see first fruits modeled. It is not a set percentage, but it is the best and first gleaning of your crops or of what you make.

We see offerings modeled in Exodus 35:29.

"All the Israelite men and women who were willing brought to the LORD freewill offerings for all the work the LORD through Moses had commanded them to do."

Once again it is not a set percentage and it's an above-and-beyond gift.

With first fruits and offerings, our motivation is to practice generosity and express gratefulness. God often responds with additional blessings over us.

A simple way of practicing this type of giving might be to give a one time gift of the increase of your income, compared to your income in the previous year. It's a simple way of showing God that money does not hold your heart and you're grateful for Him supplying you with increase.

DAILY CHALLENGE: Consider the Tithe as well as First Fruits and Offerings. Have you practiced these in your generosity journey? Why or why not? If you haven't tithed before, test the Lord in this and see what happens as you stretch your faith in new ways. If you haven't given first fruits or offerings, take another step in your generosity journey by giving it a try. See how God shows up as you take your faith up a notch.

NOTES

WEEK TEN / DAY FIVE

FAITH AND FINANCES:
ENGAGING BIBLICAL GENEROSITY, PART 2

"'But when you give to the needy, do not let your left hand know what your right hand is doing,'"

MATTHEW 6:3

"Remember this: Whoever sows sparingly will also reap sparingly, and whoever sows generously will also reap generously. ⁷ Each of you should give what you have decided in your heart to give, not reluctantly or under compulsion, for God loves a cheerful giver."

2 CORINTHIANS 9:6

Today we're going to dive right in where we left off yesterday. We're looking at the different types of giving we see in scripture. Yesterday we covered the first two, the Tithe and First Fruits and Offerings.

The Third is: **Alms Giving**

We see Alms Giving described in Matthew 6:2-4:
² "'So when you give to the needy, do not announce it with trumpets, as the hypocrites do in the synagogues and on the streets, to be honored by others. Truly I tell you, they have received their reward in full. ³ But when you give to the needy, do not let your left hand know what your right hand is doing, ⁴ so that your giving may be in secret. Then your Father, who sees what is done in secret, will reward you.'"

This is the type of giving that we often think of when we talk about giving to the poor. It's about meeting the needs of the poor and lowly. It is the type of giving that is meant to be done in secret. It's about protecting people's dignity in their crisis.

Jesus makes a big deal about not boasting about your generosity when giving to the poor, so as much as I love telling stories it would not seem appropriate to share a story at this time. But I will say, I've been on the giving end of this type of generosity as well as the receiving end. As the receiver, it was humbling, but also overwhelming. Not in such a way that I felt the love of the giver, but more so, how I felt the love of God. I felt seen by God in my time of greatest need.

Our motivation is compassion, sympathy, and love and **God's response** is a provision of private joy, as well as rewards we will receive in heaven.

There are lots of ways you can step into this type of generosity right now. You can give to local food banks or homeless shelters. You can give to a friend who you know is in need. Be creative in how you can give anonymously. My family sponsors a boy through Compassion International. In doing so, we help meet the needs of a child who lives in poverty. If you're married, talk it over with your spouse about how you can give to the poor. If you have kids, talk with them about how to give financially to those in need as well as how to personally serve the poor. There are many organizations that your family can go and serve with. It will be a blessing to those you serve, and will be life-changing for your family as well.

The final form of Biblical giving is: **Seed Sowing**

In 2 Corinthians 9:6 Paul says, "Remember this: Whoever sows sparingly will also reap sparingly, and whoever sows generously will also reap generously."

Consider the parable of the sower. In the parable, the sower is sowing seeds of the Gospel. I believe one of the greatest ways to financially sow is to invest dollars in organizations and individuals who are proclaiming the Gospel. You are providing seed money that is being used to spread the Gospel.

Our motivation is purposefully sowing into the work of the Gospel and the Word of God. We see **God's response** in the parable of the sower. It is a harvest of 30, 60, or 100-fold in fruit (people who accept Jesus as their Savior).

Here's a couple ways you can do this. You can give to a missionary, or a ministry outside of your local church. You can support a local Christian Radio station or a missions organization overseas. You can give to an organization that translates the Bible into different languages and helps distribute them to unreached people groups. There are lots of ways to sow into the spread of the Gospel. Take a step into it today.

In the end, everything we've talked about this week is about our walk with God, loving Him more, and growing our faith. It is not a calculated manipulation of God's financial principles. As we started this week, we end this week: God wants your heart. He knows your heart is connected to your treasure, so consider how you can generously use your earthy treasure for Him.

DAILY CHALLENGE: As you consider Alms Giving and Seed Sowing, have you practiced these in your generosity journey? Why or why not? How is God calling you today to take another step in your giving?

NOTES

WEEK TEN / DAY SIX & SEVEN

What idea was most challenging this week?

What day or concept do you want to rethink about?

NOTES

WEEK ELEVEN

FAITH AND RELATIONSHIPS: WE ARE TRUTH TELLERS

"Therefore each of you must put off falsehood and speak truthfully to your neighbor, for we are all members of one body."

EPHESIANS 4:25

"Be kind and compassionate to one another, forgiving each other, just as in Christ God forgave you."

EPHESIANS 4:32

Years ago there was a social experiment that was captured on video. The conductors of the experiment had people stand face to face and stare into each other's eyes without talking for four minutes. The people who were paired up were not random but had relationships with each other. They were husband-wife, father-daughter, mother-son, sisters, brothers, best friends, etc. As they stare, the four minutes seem like an eternity. They all start with nervous movements, some giggle, others smile. But as the time goes by, something shifts. Their faces turn to significant and deep expressions of emotion. Tears start to well up in the eyes of the pairs. It's as if just staring into each other's eyes they start to really see each other. They see the greater significance of the relationship. And what we witness is repentance, forgiveness, reconciliation, appreciation, building each other up, love and grace, etc.—all these things start to happen.

Beneath the busyness and hectic realities of our world, there are people. If we could slow down enough to see the significance in our brothers and sisters in this family of God, we would probably see the importance in getting our relationships right.

In Ephesians 4:25-32, the Apostle Paul speaks directly to behaviors that are necessary to "win" in our relationships. One might ask, "How do our faith and our relationships tie together?" If you've ever had a broken relationship, you know how deeply tied they are. You know how, apart from the supernatural work of God, this relationship will remain broken. You've prayed for understanding. You've prayed for reconciliation. You've prayed for forgiveness. We find ourselves praying and praying and praying... Why? Because we know how broken humanity can become. We know how desperately we need a touch from God upon our relationships.

This week we will put purposeful direction behind our faith-filled prayers. We want to take leaps of faith toward each other and toward building healthy relationships. For many of us, this week may feel like the scariest and biggest leaps are being taken with God and with one another. We are going to be desperately relying on God to take our obedience and faith and produce healing, wholeness, and prosperity in our relationships.

We will jump into this with the end result in mind. In verse 32, Paul ends with this as the final outcome in our relationships. He says, "Be kind and compassionate to one another, forgiving each other, just as in Christ God forgave you."

Isn't that how we want every relationship to be? A relationship filled with kindness and compassion for one another. I think every one of us would agree, that's what we want. So how do we get there? The Apostle Paul hits a handful of crucial behaviors that we must embrace to lead us to that end. This week we're going to consider these behaviors and in faith take a step toward them.

The first behavior is this: **We Are Truth Tellers.**

In verse 25 Paul says, "Therefore each of you must put off falsehood and speak truthfully to your neighbor, for we are all members of one body."

I think it's obvious that we shouldn't deceive people, but truth telling is more than that. It's a willingness to say that which is difficult but truthful.

My wife and I recently saw one of our childhood "rockstar" icons in concert. The now 60-year-old-rockstar was not what he was back in the day. The band sounded amazing, the light show was extraordinary, but his vocals were just not quite there. If I would have tweeted about the concert I probably would have tagged it this way, #autotunecantsavethis,

#pastyourprime, #hasanyonetoldyouthetruth. In fact, that's the one comment Lisa and I made to each other multiple times throughout the night. We would say, "Surely he knows," "surely someone has told him," "surely someone loves him enough to tell him the truth".

When it comes to building healthy relationships, truth is one of its cornerstones.

It does the relationship no good to bury the problems, to not express true feelings, or to ignore the issues. Now when it comes to truth telling, here's something to keep in mind: **your "truth" is not always true.** Meaning, you can express how you truly are feeling (that's telling the truth), but your feelings may be completely unwarranted (they are not based on truth). We see this all the time as parents.

A child comes running up to us in tears saying, "so and so is being mean to me." They are expressing how they truly feel. But when we call the other sibling in and ask what happened, the other sibling explains the situation and they ended up NOT being in the wrong at all and they were not being mean, their sibling just misinterpreted the situation. That is what was actually true.

But if we are truth tellers, we will be able to sort through what was misinterpretation, miscommunication, or simply a mistake. It takes some time, some patience, and a lot of understanding. But the healthiest relationships seek truth.

Who do you need to speak truthfully to? Is there someone close to you acting inappropriately and no one is calling them out? Are you the one who could be a truth teller in their life? Would they receive it from you? Is there a family member who is just "off" and someone needs to be a truth teller to them?

Speaking the truth can be an incredibly daunting task, but it's worth stepping into.

Let me give you one piece of advice if you take a step into truth telling with someone today. Yes, tell them the truth, but here's how to deliver it.

Say, "I could be wrong, but this is how I feel…" or "I could be wrong, but this is my perception…"

What you're doing is setting the conversation up with humility and love. To say "I could be wrong" is a posture of humility. To say "this is how I feel" or "my perception" is setting the right foundation for the conversation. It's recognizing that you're not the final say or perfect judge over the situation. It's your feelings and perceptions which may or may not be true, but you're communicating that you're in pursuit of truth and seeking to discover if your feelings or perceptions are warranted.

DAILY CHALLENGE: Is there someone in your life that you believe you need to speak the truth to in love? Is there a best way to approach the conversation? Make sure your heart is in the right place. Don't approach the conversation from hurt, but from humility and love. Finally, pray… pray… pray. I know many people would say, "if I say this, it would take a miracle." Yep, that's why this is the faith experiment. Engage your faith in this process. We need the author of all relationships to show up in our relationships. How do you want to see Him work in your relationships today?

NOTES

FAITH AND RELATIONSHIPS:
WE DON'T LET ANGER LINGER

[26] ""In your anger do not sin': Do not let the sun go down while you are still angry, [27] and do not give the devil a foothold."

EPHESIANS 4:26-27

I'm definitely not a perfect person. I've hurt people, just like all of us have. The most heartbreaking hurts are when I find out someone has felt hurt for a long time and I was completely unaware.

I had a conversation not too long ago with an individual who had been carrying anger toward me for years. The bizarre part was their anger toward me was over something I had never said or done. They believed I had a specific thought about them, which I didn't. So for years they were harboring anger toward me over nothing.

When they finally shared their feelings with me, it was amazing how quickly years of pain seemed to melt away. When I told them that I had never had that thought about them or felt that way toward them, their anger dissipated on the spot. In fact, they felt pretty silly that they had been carrying all this unwarranted anger toward me all these years.

What a waste of emotion, time, and energy over something that wasn't what they thought it was.

Yet this is the story of all anger.

Even anger that is warranted is usually given way too much unhealthy emotion, time, and energy. What would happen in your relationships if your anger wasn't given time and space to linger?

This is the second behavior: **We Don't Let Anger Linger.**

In Ephesians 4:26 the Apostle Paul says, "In your anger do not sin."

Feelings of anger are not always wrong. But what you do with your anger matters. How you deal with or don't deal with your anger will set you up for healing or give the devil a foothold in your life.

I've heard people say, "even Jesus got angry" and that the Bible talks about righteous anger, so some forms of anger are okay. To which I reply, "You're right, Jesus handled it rightly every time. But He is God and I am not. I can trust Him to live in it rightly, but I don't trust myself to live in it rightly, so I will default to dealing with it quickly."

Overall, I treat anger like going to the dentist, not like going to the spa. I aim to get the work done quickly and efficiently and get out. My goal is not to linger and sit in it for longer than I need to.

Paul speaks to that point by going on to say, *"Do not let the sun go down while you are still angry."*

Anger is a time-sensitive emotion.
I think God knew that **anger + time = bad outcomes.**
Those bad outcomes are bitterness, rage, unforgiveness, gossip, slander and the like.
The better equation is **anger + a quick direct approach = freedom.**

If you deal with anger quickly, you're free from carrying emotional burdens and inaccurate perspectives for extended periods of time. You're free from turning hypothetical conversations over and over in your head that will never happen. You're free from the paranoia of what others may or may not be feeling. You're free because you faced it and dealt with your anger quickly.

The Apostle Paul says deal with your anger quickly and "do not give the devil a foothold." The Greek word for foothold can literally be translated as "space." How would you respond if I asked it this way? Are you okay with giving the devil just a little bit of space in your life?

Well of course not. Even a little bit of space is too much space for the devil to have in any of our lives.

If you own a house, picture it this way. Would you be okay having a robber live in the attic of your home? He's just a robber. And he's there to steal as much from your house as he can. But he's currently only in the attic. Is it cool if he stays there, as long as he doesn't come out of the attic too often? As long as he hides away, we can all just ignore him.

This is what many of us do with anger. We hide it away and pretend it's not there. But all the while it's stealing from other places in the home.

We can not continue to live this way. We would never ignore the robber and we should not ignore our anger.

Along with this, we can't talk about anger without talking about forgiveness. Almost all our anger stems from hurts. And when it involves relationships, those hurts need forgiveness.

Paul ends in verse 32 by saying, "forgiving each other, just as in Christ God forgave you."

Christ offered us forgiveness before we were sorry and without any conditions. We are called to forgive according to His standard. That is regardless of their response and without conditions. It's always easier to forgive when the person who hurt us is sorry, but we need to be committed to forgiveness according to the Jesus standard. That is, I will offer forgiveness regardless of their response. And I will offer forgiveness without conditions.

It starts with a conscious choice. It's a choice to do what God is calling us to do even when we don't feel like it. What I've discovered about forgiveness is that the heart always follows the obedient mind. We have to choose to think rightly even before our heart feels rightly. We make the mental choice to forgive, and if you do that enough times in obedience to God, you'll find that one day your heart has caught up with your thinking.

I picture it like a deep wound. If you get a deep cut, you don't just throw a bandaid on it and wake up the next day with it completely healed. No, you clean the cut daily and care for the wound. You would probably do that for quite some time until eventually the wound heals. In the same way, when we forgive, we are cleaning and tending that emotional wound. If we do it rightly over time, one day you'll discover the wound is fully healed. And along the way, anger was not given any space to rob you in your life.

DAILY CHALLENGE: This day may engage your faith in a degree that is greater than anything you've done so far. You might think it would take a miracle for "this" or "that" relationship that has been wounded in anger to be healed. Today is the day to take a leap of faith and deal with your anger. Who do you need to forgive? If your anger is toward a family member, you probably need to take this beyond your alone time with Jesus. You probably need to have a conversation with the person. It's time to pray, pray, pray. It's time for healing. It's time to deal with your anger.

NOTES

"Anyone who has been stealing must steal no longer, but must work, doing something useful with their own hands, that they may have something to share with those in need."

EPHESIANS 4:28

There is nothing worse than feeling alone when trying to tackle a huge project. I've been in that situation many times. I've got the entire yard to rake and no one is helping me. I've got the entire basement to clean (none of it is my mess) and no one is helping. I've got whatever the huge project is, and no one is helping. It's amazing how quickly those situations can cause relational tension. I find myself frustrated, hurt or angry because others aren't contributing.

The third relational behavior is just that: **We Contribute.**

Ephesians 4:28 says everyone "must work, doing something useful with their own hands, that they may have something to share with those in need."

This is all about being a contributor to those we have relationships with. No one likes a one-sided, life-sucking relationship. We long for mutually beneficial and mutually giving relationships. We want relationships with a healthy give and take.

Unfortunately, it's easy to take advantage of relationships over time. For example, my wife has been doing our laundry for most of our marriage. I'll try every once in a while, but honestly, my folding of the laundry is not even close to how well she does it. So, it's easy for me to just let her do it. But then it's also easy for me to say nothing about it.

She's bringing something to the relationship that is actually a great contribution. I think one of the strategies of the enemy is to block our awareness of others' contributions. If the devil can keep us distracted enough in our own world, we may not see all the ways that others are actually trying to serve us. We may miss out on how others are trying to invest in the relationship or show their love and support to us.

Another way of saying we contribute could be to say, we make an effort, we try.

Sometimes the greatest thing you can do in any relationship is simply make an effort. Give it a try. Try to be romantic. Make an effort to play with your kid. Try to help your spouse with their chores. Make an effort to have a conversation with your teen. Make an effort to lead your family in a devotional time (reading the Bible). Make an effort to pray with your spouse.

G.K. Chesterton once said it this way, **"If it's something worth doing, then it's worth doing poorly."** It's the idea that putting forth any effort (even a poor effort) into the right thing is worth it, over no effort at all.

Here's where faith comes in. In faith, I often pray that God will produce something with my effort that is bigger than I can see or imagine.

For example if I'm serving my kids, it does me no good to say to them, "Don't you see how much I love you by the way I'm serving you?" But I can pray, "God help my kids to see my love for them by the way I'm serving them. Help my kids to see a model of servanthood that they may follow."

Here's the other way faith is often a part of this behavior. More often than not, we need supernatural strength to contribute or to even want to try.

How often have you thought, "I've got nothing left in the tank"? Probably more than we would like to admit. But relationships take time and they take effort. And when you feel burnt out and exhausted, effort is often a miracle in itself. So we need supernatural strength to even be able to have anything to give.

I pray regularly, "God give me strength to do that which I am too tired to do. God, help me to give to my relationships when I feel lazy or when I feel apathetic. God, help me to try when I don't feel like trying."

Relationships are always worth investing in and giving to, but we often need the power of God to produce that in us.

DAILY CHALLENGE: What things do you take for granted in your relationships? Is there a relationship you've gotten lazy in? What could you do today to contribute to that relationship? Are there places in your relationships where you know you just need to make an effort? Ask for supernatural strength to give more than you can give, and for God to use that effort in the relationship.

NOTES

....

....

....

....

....

....

....

....

....

....

....

"Do not let any unwholesome talk come out of your mouths, but only what is helpful for building others up according to their needs, that it may benefit those who listen."

EPHESIANS 4:29

I regularly have people come up to me and give me a word of encouragement. It could be how God has used me in their life or how God has used Lakeland (our church) in their spiritual journey. Those words of encouragement are always sweet to hear and I praise God for them. However, those words are not the same as a word of encouragement from my wife. If she says something encouraging it carries an entirely different weight to it. Same thing for my kids. If they say something encouraging to me, I know it's a BIG deal. And what they say will leave a real impact upon me. Why do my family's words mean more to me than a stranger's? Because they are my closest relationships.

This describes the importance of our fourth relational behavior:
We Speak Life.

Now, we've talked about the power of life and death in our tongues before, but now consider the profound impact that can have on your closest relationships. There is a unique dynamic in the power of our words with our closest friends and closest relationships.

I believe God knows of this power which is why He encourages us to speak "only what is helpful for building others up according to their needs, that it may benefit those who listen."

While, of course, this can be applied to any relationship, I believe it can be life-altering when applied to our closest relationships.

Here's a simple way I apply it with my daughters. When addressing my daughters I will often say, "Hey, beautiful." I want to speak that over them and speak it over them often. Why? Because culture and social media is constantly attacking their self image. It's not that I want them to be proud of their beauty. I want them to know they are beautiful just as God created them. I want to speak life over their identities and help build an identity in them that is true.

It's funny how sometimes saying words of encouragement can sometimes feel forced or unnatural. I think the enemy lies to us and says, "If you say it, it will just feel forced." So we say nothing. But honestly, even if it feels forced, who cares? Just like I said yesterday, if it's worth doing, it's worth doing poorly. It's better to say anything that is life-giving, even if it feels forced, then say nothing at all.

How could you do this?

Here are a few things we've done in our home. We've called our kids by the meanings of their names for a season of time. All of our kids' names have pretty cool meanings. They mean things like, divine play, brave, fire, powerful commander, delight, etc. For a little while, instead of calling our kids by their names, I would call them "brave one," "fiery one," "powerful commander." The point is, there is something powerful about speaking these identities over them.

We've also written words of encouragement, declarations, or verses over our kids and written those in places where they would see them regularly. You could do this by writing with a dry erase marker on a mirror that your friend or family member uses regularly.

Get creative, but get after it. Speak life. No matter how awkward or forced it feels, those words of life will be powerful in shaping your relationships.

DAILY CHALLENGE: Write down the names of your five closest relationships. They may be family members or close friends. Now ask God to give you a word or phrase that you can speak over them. Once you have your words or phrases, get creative in how you can speak that over them regularly. Let's pray faith-filled prayers that God would use these words and phrases to shape their lives for His kingdom.

"Get rid of all bitterness, rage and anger, brawling and slander, along with every form of malice."

EPHESIANS 4:31

I don't know how it happens but it happens every year and it happens pretty regularly. Birds find their way into our church building. It drives me crazy to see birds flying around our foyer space or in an auditorium. Mostly because I don't want them to "go to the bathroom" in our building. Can you imagine being at a worship service and getting bird doodoo dropped on you? That's not the touch from God you were looking for. So what do I do? I get rid of the bird. I'm like a hunter who will not let up till that thing is out of our building. What's crazy to me is some of our staff will say, "Don't worry about it, just leave it alone, it will find its way out." Don't worry about it!? What?

Just leave it alone!?

It will find its way out!?

Are you kidding me? If this was happening in your own home, would you say those things? If there was a bird flying around your family room, would you just go about your day, not worry about it, leave it alone, and hope it finds its way out? Of course not! If it was your home, you wouldn't stop chasing the bird around your house until you got it out.

Why? Because you know it cannot be allowed to stay there.

Today's fifth behavior speaks to something that cannot be tolerated: **We Do Not Tolerate Destructive Language.**

When I say destructive language, I'm not talking about cursing. I'm talking about hurtful words of anger, bitterness and slander. Unfortunately, some have allowed destructive language to be present in their relationships.

The Apostle Paul speaks bluntly to these behaviors when he says in Ephesians 4:31 to "Get rid of all bitterness, rage and anger, brawling and slander, along with every form of malice."

Unfortunately, these are many of the behaviors that are acceptable and modeled in our culture today. The world fights manipulatively, it fights rudely, it fights unfair and selfishly.

The word that gets translated as "get rid of" is *Airo* and it can be translated as "to carry away." It's like taking out the trash. We've got to carry away this form of trash that has worked its way into our relationships.

How have destructive forms of language worked their way into your relationships? In women it can often be passive aggressive language. It's an unfair way of using your words to "play the martyr" or "play the victim." In men it can often be domineering, bullying, or intimidating in their language. Using threats or ultimatums to get their way. Or course, these behaviors can apply to anyone. But they often do apply to specific genders that way because they were modeled to us that way.

Maybe you use your words in one of these destructive ways. Today is the day that you acknowledge it and agree not to tolerate it, even in yourself.

As you choose to not tolerate unhealthy past behaviors, you're going to need God in this. It probably won't be surprising how often you'll go back to unhealthy patterns that you've spent years establishing. We need the Holy Spirit's reminder, conviction, strength and wisdom as we establish new behaviors with our words. This will be a really practical place to see your faith in action as God produces something new in you.

Our relationships matter to God and they should really matter to us. He's given us some clear instructions on how to protect, support and safeguard our relationships. This week we've added some solid behaviors to our relationships and with the help of God, He will help produce the richest and sweetest relationships in our lives.

Do you currently tolerate unhealthy language in your relationships? Do you have any destructive behaviors in how you use your words in your relationships? Do you need to confess and repent to a friend or family member about how you've done this? Talk it over with someone. What new habits can you put in your life to replace the old? What is God calling you to do today to strengthen your relationships?

NOTES

DAY 6: LET THAT THOUGHT SIMMER

What idea was most challenging this week?

DAY 7: LET THAT THOUGHT SIMMER

What day or concept do you want to rethink about?

WEEK TWELVE

WEEK TWELVE / DAY ONE

FAITH AND POWER: THE CONNECTION OF OUR WITNESS AND POWER

"'But you will receive power when the Holy Spirit comes on you; and you will be my witnesses in Jerusalem, and in all Judea and Samaria, and to the ends of the earth.'"

ACTS 1:8

[18] "I will not venture to speak of anything except what Christ has accomplished through me in leading the Gentiles to obey God by what I have said and done— [19] by the power of signs and wonders, through the power of the Spirit of God. So from Jerusalem all the way around to Illyricum, I have fully proclaimed the gospel of Christ."

ROMANS 15:18-19

[4] "My message and my preaching were not with wise and persuasive words, but with a demonstration of the Spirit's power, [5] so that your faith might not rest on human wisdom, but on God's power."

1 CORINTHIANS 2:4-5

Have you ever seen a magician do a live performance? Maybe I should call them an illusionist, because that's what they are. Some of my favorite YouTube videos are the ones showing an individual doing magic tricks and then their friend sitting beside them lets the cat out of the bag and grabs their trick which reveals how it was done. In one second the viewer goes from thinking, "How did they do that?" to "Ohhh… that's how they did that." It's not that amazing once you know how the trick is done.

There is an aspect to faith and a reality of who God is that is meant to leave us wondering, "how did He do that?" There is an aspect of wonder and amazement that, quite frankly, should never be satisfied.

Because we are spiritual beings with a soul, I believe there is something hard-wired into us that longs to say it is "only God." Only God can heal my broken heart. Only God can provide for my financial needs. Only God can restore my fractured relationship. Only God could have orchestrated the encounter. Only God could have done that. That was only by the POWER of God.

We long to experience something that points our hearts and minds to the One who can't fully be grasped. We long to experience a power that is not of this world and can't be explained away in a 30-second elevator pitch, because it's something so much more profound than that. It's divine in nature; supernatural.

This week we are going to be diving into the subject of Faith and Power. At the end of it all, that's what this entire journey is for. A journey to see the power of God touch different aspects of our lives. We've been pressing in with faith to see Him interact in our thinking, in our challenges, in our families, in our marriages, in our relationships, in our finances, in our workplaces and in our communities.

And this week we're going to press in a little further. If you've been stretching your faith on this journey, you have probably had some moments (hopefully many moments) when you've seen the power of God show up. The question is, are the "only God" moments meant to be few and far between? Are they only for the most religious, or the most spiritual people? Are they only for seasons like now when reading this book? Where do these "only God" moments fit in the rhythm of our lives?

As long as we don't put down our faith Monday through Saturday and only pick it back up on Sundays for a brief hour, I believe our lives are meant to be saturated with "only God" moments. **We are not people who just talk about God, but our lives are the canvas for the constant display of the power of God.**

Consider some of our scripture for today.

"'<u>But you will receive power</u> when the Holy Spirit comes on you; and you will be my witnesses in Jerusalem, and in all Judea and Samaria, and to the ends of the earth.'"

ACTS 1:8

¹⁸ "I will not venture to speak of anything except what Christ has accomplished through me in leading the Gentiles to obey God by what I have said and done— ¹⁹ <u>by the power of signs and wonders, through the power of the Spirit of God.</u>"

ROMANS 15:18-19A

⁴ "My message and my preaching were not with wise and persuasive words, <u>but with a demonstration of the Spirit's power,</u> ⁵ so that your faith might not rest on human wisdom, <u>but on God's power.</u>"

1 CORINTHIANS 2:4-5

I think most of us understand the idea that we need to be bold in talking about the Gospel where and when we are able. What we sometimes overlook is that our witness is meant to be accompanied by divine power. In every one of these passages it mentions both aspects. They each talk about speaking the Gospel when they say "be my witnesses," "speak of anything," "my message and my preaching." But every message is accompanied by power.

Don't miss this. The Gospel is always accompanied by power.

These two things always go side by side. They are meant to go together. Like peanut butter and jelly, milk and cookies, Batman and Robin, and Ken and Barbie, the Gospel and Power just go together.

Part of the reason why it is important that the power of God is on display in your life and in the process of sharing the gospel is touched on in 1 Corinthians 2:5.

"... so that your faith might not rest on human wisdom, but on God's power."

1 CORINTHIANS 2:5

Do you see it? Faith is not designed to rest on human wisdom. **Faith cannot simply be an intellectual exercise of what seems logical.** There is something in it that makes you go, "Wow! Only God!"

I'm not against scientific arguments, intellectual exercises, asking hard questions, and the pragmatic aspects of discussing the Gospel. I don't think we should fear those conversations or avoid them. I believe we can use logic, human reasoning and godly wisdom in our pursuit of truth. But we've got to realize that faith can't rest solely on those things.

There is something, that apart from the power of God, "shouldn't add up" in the mind of any of us.

Let me give you a scenario to think through. This was a situation I talked through with one of my former students (turned pastor) years ago. He was an intellectually heavy thinker and I wanted to challenge him in his approach to the gospel. We walked into a coffee shop and I proposed a challenge. I pointed to a random gal who was sitting alone at a table and drinking her coffee. I asked my friend how he would try to broach the subject of the gospel or go about trying to share the gospel with her. He talked through a handful of strategies on how to start up a spiritual conversation that might lead to sharing the gospel. He talked through how to reason with her depending on her spiritual perspective. He talked and reasoned and reasoned and talked. Then he asked me, "How would you handle it?"

I looked at her, then back at him and said, "Do you see her hand?" She was wearing a splint on her wrist. I said, "I would go over and ask what happened to her hand. After listening, I would ask if I can pray for healing over her hand. Then, if God touched her hand in some form or fashion, that touch will do more than anything I can say. If there is no change or any immediate outcome, I would share a couple stories with her of individuals that I've prayed for who have experienced healing. I would connect their stories to the greatest story in history. The story of the great healer (Jesus) who came to heal and fix our broken relationship with God."

I've actually done this many times. I rarely try to argue anyone to Jesus; it's far easier to show them the power of Jesus when I pray for whatever situation they are facing.

Here's my reasoning: if it worked for the Apostle Paul, it can work for me. Why would I try to invent a different or "more effective" way for people to encounter God and the gospel? Paul's success rate with this method is pretty compelling.

Today, think about who God has placed in your sphere of influence. Instead of feeling like you've got to say all the right things to lead them to Jesus, perhaps all you need to do is look for an opportunity where you can pray for God's power to show up in their lives. Don't feel bad placing the weight of the gospel on the shoulders of God showing up in someone's life. He can handle that weight. He's more concerned about their faith journey than we are. So set Him up to show up and show off.

DAILY CHALLENGE: Who in your sphere of influence do you think is a spiritual seeker (open to talking about God)? Instead of trying to say the right thing, consider how God would lead you to pray the right thing with them. Try it out: ask them today, "How can I pray for you?" Or if you know their situation (struggles), take a minute to pray with them for what they are facing. Pray a big faith-filled prayer that requires God to show up in their lives. Then follow up with them later and ask if they saw God work in any unique way in their situation.

NOTES

FAITH AND POWER:
POWER FOR THE SPIRITUAL BATTLE

"For our struggle is not against flesh and blood, but against the rulers, against the authorities, against the powers of this dark world and against the spiritual forces of evil in the heavenly realms."

EPHESIANS 6:12

"The weapons we fight with are not the weapons of the world. On the contrary, they have divine power to demolish strongholds."

2 CORINTHIANS 10:4

When Lisa and I lived in Minnesota we had a pretty difficult situation with one of our neighbors. It was beyond a normal neighborly disagreement. They were outright hostile to us. They would hover by their back windows and doors and if a child crossed over the property line they would yell at them. They would scowl and stare, and periodically curse and shout at us. They would blame us for things that seemed way off base. We always felt like it was spiritual in nature, as if our property line literally backed up to the gates of hell. In one of our last encounters with that neighbor, the mom yelled at us for the way our dog barked constantly. At that point we knew beyond a shadow of doubt that it was a spiritual battle as our dog had passed away a year and a half before. The enemy is usually very subtle, but on that occasion, he was just outright blatant. And we were in a full-on spiritual war.

We felt like we needed reinforcements and additional support, so I asked some members of our prayer team to come over to our house and pray. About 10 of us gathered together to pray. We had a lot to cover as we prayed over each child and each room. But when it came to our property, one of the prayer team members said, "I feel like we should walk around your property seven times like Joshua did with the people of Israel. In the same way that God won that physical battle, let's pray God brings us the spiritual battle over this space." Because things had gotten so crazy, I was open to anything. March around our house seven times… sure, I'm up for that. So that's what we did. I remember hoping no one saw us as we walked around our property that night in the dark, because they would definitely think we were a cult. But at that point, if I'm honest, I really didn't care what anyone thought. We were in a spiritual battle.

You'll never guess what happened next. Within the week our neighbors had put their house on the market and within the month they had moved out. Now, I'm not suggesting if you want to get rid of your neighbors, start marching around your property. But I am suggesting that there is real power accessible for the children of God that we need to learn to use to fight spiritual battles.

This is a key place where you are meant to see the power of God on display.

In Ephesians 6, Paul states that our battles that we face are not against flesh and blood, but they are spiritual battles. I think many of us think the way I did with my neighbor in Minnesota. "They are just mean," or "for whatever reason we just don't get along," but rarely do we think "this is a spiritual attack."

I believe there is a spiritual dynamic to every one of our physical encounters. And in 2 Corinthians 10:4 the Apostle Paul says, "The weapons we fight with are not the weapons of the world. On the contrary, they have divine power to demolish strongholds."

Paul says we have divine power to demolish these spiritual strongholds. We desperately need the power of God because many of the things we face are not just human arguments or human conflict, they are spiritual strongholds.

I don't mean to imply that there is a demon hiding behind every bush, lurking and looking for the moment they can jump out and grab you. However, while the enemy may not be hiding behind a bush, he likely is hiding behind the lie that you've believed. He is likely hiding behind the confusion that is ruling in your workplace. He is hiding behind the gossip in the breakroom. He is hiding behind the fear that you've embraced. And he is hiding behind that childhood trauma that still haunts you to this day.

But the work of God in our lives is not just to create a better outlook in life. It's not just so we can say, "God saved me and now my life can be a little better than it was before." Yes, it can be better. But it's beyond just getting a little better, it's about wholeness and freedom. It's about how the gospel and power truly go together. And **His power can break down every spiritual stronghold that has come against you.**

How can you identify if there is a spiritual battle going on in a situation? Let me point to three assessments.

1. **The flavor of the fruit.**
   What I mean by this is, we refer to the fruit of the Spirit as love, joy, peace, patience, kindness, etc. The fruit of the flesh (and the fruit of the enemy) is the opposite of those: anger, frustration, impatience, gossip, slander, fear. Ask yourself, what is on display? If the situation you are in is permeated by anger, frustration, impatience, gossip, slander, fear, etc., there is a spiritual battle at hand.

2. **Lies.**
   You can identify this when you hear someone say something that is an outright lie. It can be about someone or something. But behind the lie is the liar (Satan). Wherever lies are spread there is a spiritual battle at hand.

3. **Confusion.**
   You can see it when there seems to be chaos, complete miscommunication and misunderstanding, or a lack of direction or clarity. I've been in community meetings where something is trying to be accomplished and then someone gets up and vents their frustrations. They hop from subject to subject, hitting on things that are sort of related, yet not really related to the purpose at hand. The next thing you know, people are weighing in on the vast array of things that were vented. An hour later someone asks, "What are we talking about again?" The meeting has gone so long, they decide to adjourn and pick it up again next month.

When this happens, one of the simplest things you can do is start praying.

Pray that God would break the power of the enemy in that situation. Pray that the angry person would be silenced, the lie would be exposed, or that confusion would be dispelled. Pray that peace would reign, truth would be seen, and clarity would come.

Your faith was made to be accompanied by power. That power is made to win spiritual battles. Will you take your faith into the battle today?

DAILY CHALLENGE: What difficulty or hurdle are you facing? Is there a spiritual battle raging there? Put it through the three assessments. How can you pray and engage in the spiritual battle for this situation? Finally, if you are overwhelmed by the battle, ask your small group to join you, or ask for support from your church's prayer team. But don't feel like you have to do it alone. The family of God is a team sport, and watching the power of God win spiritual battles is fun to do as a team as well.

NOTES

WEEK TWELVE / DAY THREE

FAITH AND POWER:
DON'T UNDERESTIMATE THE POWER

"I pray that the eyes of your heart may be enlightened in order that you may know the hope to which he has called you, the riches of his glorious inheritance in his holy people, [19] and his incomparably great power for us who believe. That power is the same as the mighty strength [20] he exerted when he raised Christ from the dead and seated him at his right hand in the heavenly realms."

EPHESIANS 1:18-20

Years ago, I prayed throughout one week that God would give me a unique gift from Him. I was preaching about how God can show His love to us in unique and personal ways that only we might see. Sometimes those expressions of love from God come in unique packages. I wasn't quite ready for what He gave me. I had been praying and praying all week long that God would give me something that was so astounding, it would shock me, wow me, and that it would be a mind-blowing gift to me. At the end of the week, on that Saturday, Lisa and I found out she was pregnant. It was definitely not something we were planning for or trying for, but nonetheless, she was pregnant.

I couldn't help but just laugh. That's not what I had in mind at all for God shocking me and wowing me, but that definitely did it. Because I had been praying for a sweet gift from God to me, I couldn't help but see the pregnancy through that lens. It's not that the gift was not for both of us, but this little life felt like it was specifically for me.

So I was confused and heartbroken when Lisa called me and said, "I'm losing the baby, I've started bleeding and cramping." This didn't make sense. This baby was a gift from God to me.

I came home, hugged my wife and told her, "No matter what happens,

God is good and it will be okay." I went upstairs to our bedroom and just sat on the bed and I started praying. I prayed all I knew how to pray. I prayed a prayer of surrender, surrendering the situation to him. I prayed thanksgiving prayers, simply giving thanks for who He is and what He's done in our lives. I prayed "not my will, but yours be done."

But then I felt like the Lord led me to pray a different prayer. I felt like the Lord asked me, "Do you really believe I can do anything? Then really pray that way."

So I did. I prayed, "God, stop the bleeding, touch Lisa's body, protect this baby, and save this little one's life." I prayed, "God, display the power of the resurrected Christ right now."

I came downstairs and repeated to Lisa what I had said to her before. "No matter what happens, God is good and it will be okay." It wasn't a half hour later that Lisa came to me and said, "my cramping has stopped and so has the bleeding." The following day Lisa had a doctor's appointment and it was confirmed that the baby was okay.

I don't know if it was my prayers that made a difference or if Lisa just had some random complications early in the pregnancy. All I know is how I prayed and how I felt like the Lord was wanting to grow my faith during that season. He wanted my faith to match what I theologically believed about Him. He wanted me to pray ridiculous resurrection prayers, even when they made no sense.

The first chapter of Ephesians describes some of the most mind blowing ideas that apply to Christians. The Apostle Paul is praying that we would know "his incomparably great power for us who believe. That power is the same as the mighty strength he exerted when he raised Christ from the dead and seated him at his right hand in the heavenly realms."

He's literally praying that we would experience resurrection-type power in our lives. I think often we undershoot and underestimate the power of God. We pray prayers that don't require much faith at all.

I know I've said this before. While I never want to boss God around, I also never want to be afraid to ask for that which the cross accomplished. In fact, I believe it's our responsibility to ask for that which the cross made possible.

I never want to short-sell His power, underestimate what He can do, or undermine His ability.

I want my faith to match the capacity of the cross.

DAILY CHALLENGE: Do you have a tendency to underestimate His power? Why? How does God want to stretch your faith today? What would resurrection prayers sound like when applied to situations in your life?

NOTES

WEEK TWELVE / DAY FOUR

FAITH AND POWER:
WE'RE NOT WORTHY

"But he said to me, 'My grace is sufficient for you, for my power is made perfect in weakness.' Therefore I will boast all the more gladly about my weaknesses, so that Christ's power may rest on me."

2 CORINTHIANS 12:9

I don't know if you ever watched the "Saturday Night Live" skits with Wayne's World. The two characters, Wayne and Garth, had some pretty epic catchphrases. One of them was "We're not worthy! We're not worthy!" They would have a guest star on the episode, and upon their arrival Wayne and Garth would immediately start chanting in sync with one another, "We're not worthy!"

I think that's how a lot of us feel in regard to the power of God. We may Biblically believe that God has the power, and even that the power is available, but in the end we don't ask God for much because "we're not worthy."

Have you felt this way? You may not feel righteous enough, or like you know enough, or like you're "Christian enough" to ask for God to display His power in and through you.

The Apostle Paul was one of those guys who probably felt unworthy. That's right, Paul. Why? Because before Paul became the greatest New Testament missionary, he was a Christian killer. He captured, persecuted, tortured and killed Christians. If there was ever someone who didn't feel worthy, Paul understood those feelings.

Because of those feelings God had to do some special care in Paul's life and bring a special message just for Paul to work through his feelings of inadequacy.

Paul describes what God spoke directly to him to help him get past this hurdle. In 2 Corinthians 12:9 Paul says, "But he (God) said to me, 'My grace is sufficient for you, for my power is made perfect in weakness.'"

God saw how weak and unworthy Paul felt. As a result God speaks to that feeling of inadequacy and says to Paul, that's okay, "my power is made perfect in weakness." Meaning, it's perfect that Paul feels weak, for the following reason: **When God shows up and displays His power in weak people, you'll never mistake who did the work.** The individual will know beyond a shadow of a doubt that they had nothing to do with it. It also continually reinforces God's upside down kingdom where He takes the least, the lowest, and the unworthy and displays the most and the greatest in them.

If you feel weak, inadequate and unworthy, you are a perfect candidate for the power of God to be displayed in. That's God's plan for His display of power. Use weak people to display His strength. Our problem is that we get really nervous about the plan. We don't want to look foolish praying for things and then they don't happen.

So what do we do? We don't pray resurrection-power type prayers, we pray prayers that keep us in our comfort zone. Someone once said, "Comfort zones don't keep your life safe. They keep it small."

If you're like me, you want to live life large. You don't want to settle for small faith and small power. So don't allow weakness, unworthiness, or inadequacy stop you. Embrace the reality that God uses people who feel that way.

Let's declare the same thing Paul said, "Therefore I will boast all the more gladly about my weaknesses, so that Christ's power may rest on me."

DAILY CHALLENGE: Where do you feel unworthy, inadequate, or weak? Let's ask God to use the places where we feel weak to be the greatest display of His power. Let's not settle for comfort-zone faith. Let's ask for big things–not because we are worthy, but because His power is made perfect in weakness.

NOTES

FAITH AND POWER:
POWER... WHERE?

"... and through him [Jesus] to reconcile to himself [God the Father] all things, whether things on earth or things in heaven, by making peace through his blood, shed on the cross."

COLOSSIANS 1:20

Let's picture a sliding scale. On one side of the scale is the word **easy** and on the other is **difficult**. On the sliding scale, how easy or how difficult is it for God to do the following?

- heal a person
- restore a relationship
- provide financially
- break addiction
- conquer fear
- deal with anger
- offer forgiveness
- use you daily

I know it's a silly question, as you may know that the answer is always the same, and that is, they are all easy for God. Yet we pray sometimes as if some are more difficult for God. We gauge some as easier and others as more difficult for God to pull off. But they are not. There is nothing He can't do.

Colossians 1:20 tells us what the cross accomplished. It says it reconciled "to himself all things."

I often have asked, what's included in all things? ALL THINGS are included in ALL THINGS. But we often pray only for SOME THINGS, not ALL THINGS. We do it because we look at the sliding scale and we think to ourselves, "That's a big prayer, or that's a tough one." But it's not any bigger and any tougher than any other thing.

We've got to get over ourselves and our own sliding scale and be okay praying for ALL THINGS.

Consider it like a football team. Sometimes commentators will make statements like, "The offensive line made all the difference," or, "the defense saved the game," or, "if it wasn't for special teams they wouldn't have won." When you think about how a game is won, a team really needs every group that takes the field to do their part. Can you imagine if a team tried to play a game, but never played their special teams? The special teams unit does kick-offs, fourth downs, extra points, punt returns, special plays and more. Can you imagine if an NFL team completely ignored that group and didn't develop that unit? They would lose every game.

Yet, I think that's what's happened in much of the church and in many of our faith journeys. We only play half our team by only praying half the prayers. We only pray the prayers that land on the easy side of our sliding scale. As a result, we're missing half of our plays.

The cross reconciled ALL THINGS. That means God's power can touch ALL THINGS.

I can't tell you how many times I have quoted Colossians 1:20 in my prayers. It's my green light to go for the biggest, the most audacious, and the most seemingly impossible things. It's my way of reminding my heart that His power is not off limits from anything.

As we finish up the Faith Experiment, is there anything that you've placed off to the side and said, "God's power can touch most things… but not **this** or **that** thing." Today is the day to slide **all things** to the side of the scale where they belong. The easy side. They are all a part of ALL THINGS that the cross made a way to impact. Let's exercise our faith in ALL THINGS today.

DAILY CHALLENGE: As you go throughout your day, see how many things you can pray for. Everywhere you go pray for ALL THINGS as the Lord would lead you. It will truly turn into a day where you pray without ceasing. Then come back and journal. What did you pray for today that you've never prayed for before? How did the Lord lead you to pray? How has your view of His power been impacted this week?

NOTES